THE
INFA

THE GOSPEL AT INFANT BAPTISM

Frederick Levison

THE SAINT ANDREW PRESS
EDINBURGH

First published in 1980 by
THE SAINT ANDREW PRESS
121 George Street, Edinburgh EH2 4YN

ISBN 0 7152 0443 2

Printed in Great Britain by
Bell & Bain Ltd., Glasgow

'Long before they call I shall answer.'
(Isaiah 65:24, in The Jerusalem Bible)

'We love Him, because He first loved us.'
(1 John 4:19)

I take the word Sacrament...for a holy sign and seal that is annexed to the preached Word of God...Therefore the Word alone cannot be a Sacrament, nor the element alone, but Word and element must together make a Sacrament. Well has Augustine said: 'Let the Word come to the element and you shall have a Sacrament.' Thus the Word must come to the element, that is, the Word preached distinctly and opened up in all its parts must go before the Sacrament, which hangs on to it; and the Sacrament, as a seal, must follow and be appended to it. Thus I call a Sacrament the Word and Seal conjointly, the one joined on to the other.

(From a sermon preached in the Kirk of Edinburgh by Robert Bruce in 1589.)

The Westminster Confession defines that 'the visible church consists of all those throughout the world that possess the true religion, together with their children.' The children of Christian parents are received into the Church by baptism, the Church thereby declaring that the grace of God is brought to bear upon them before they themselves are conscious of its operation, and at the same time acknowledging its own responsibility for their Christian nurture – which makes it important that baptism should be administered 'in face of the congregation'. When children grow up to years of understanding a personal act of profession is expected of them, after which they are confirmed in the faith and are invited to their First Communion.

(*Report of the Commission for the Interpretation of God's Will in the Present Crisis*, presented to the General Assembly of the Church of Scotland in 1943.)

Contents

	page
Foreword	xi
Preface	xiii
Part One: FOR ANY SUNDAY	
Upside Down?	1
Unconscious Recipients	2
An Unbreakable Bond	3
Passport to Glory	4
Receiving (1)	4
Receiving (2)	5
Water Pure and Tranquil	6
What Makes a Home?	7
A New Relationship	8
In His Hands	9
Dying to Live	10
Whom is He Like	11
Jesus Loves Me	12
He Calls Them by Name	13
Beneficiaries by Faith	14
Nurture	15
The Church's One Foundation	17
The Divine Wooing	19
His Praise Shall Sound	20
A Christian Heritage	21
A New Song	22
Responding to the Gospel	23
A Startling Saying	24
The Vocation of Parenthood	25
Partings	26
Not Potters but Gardeners	27
Tell Me Who I Am	28

Latent Powers 29
Promise and Fulfilment 30
A Word for Fathers 31
A Covenant is Sealed 33
Brought to Jesus 34
A True Man 35
The Chief End of Man 36
Lent to God 37
Hannah, Samuel, and the Coat 38
Planting Well 39
A New Heart 40
The Best Gifts 41
The Value Given by Love 43
The Way the Twig is Bent 44
A Precious Memory 45
Not Just a Baby 46
The Son of a King 47
Into the Church Universal 48
The Choice is Ours 50
Mothers 51
Our Part and God's Part 52
The Moses Basket and the Courts of God 53
Family Occasions 54
Consecrating and Caring 56
Taking it Seriously 57
Loved and Valued 59
How Do You Know My Name? 60
A Magnificent Entrance to Somewhere 62
The Master's Call 63
'Baptizatus Sum' 65
A Joke That's Just Begun 66
From Generation to Generation 67
The Swallow's Nest 68
Whom Is Baptism For? 69
The Warrant 71
What a Baby Needs 72
Counting the Cost 73

The Sure Foundation 74
Earmarked 76
Make Yourself at Home 77
A Christian Home 78
'When Jesus Saw Their Faith' 79
Children are the Big Thing 81
Start Small—Stay Small 82
What is Man? 83
Procreation 84
Why in Church and not at Home? 86
Glory, Glory 87
Wild Flowers 88
More Than Meets the Eye 89
'Me Mum Will!' 90

Part Two: TIMES, SEASONS AND OCCASIONS
Advent 93
Christmas (1) 94
Christmas (2) 95
Christmas (3) 96
Christmas (4) 97
Christmas (5) 98
Christmas (6) 99
After Christmas 100
Epiphany 101
Week of Prayer for Unity 102
Palm Sunday 103
Palm Sunday (Confirmation Sunday) 104
Easter 105
Ascension Sunday (1) 106
Ascension Sunday (2) 107
Ascension Sunday (3) 108
Whitsunday 109
Whitsunday (Christian Aid Week) 110
Christian Aid Week 111

Harvest Thanksgiving 112
All Saints (1) 113
All Saints (2) 114
St Andrewstide (1) 115
St Andrewstide (2) 116
At a Children's Service 117
At a Sunday School Service 119
A Family about to Emigrate 120
A One-Parent Family 121
A Parent and Child Together 123
A Handicapped Child 124
At the End of a Ministry 125
A Prayer at the Font 127

FOREWORD

by The Very Rev. Dr G.T.H. Reid

I have great pleasure in commending this book written by Fred Levison, not only for friendship's sake, but because I believe it will supply a real need. Nothing like it, so far as I know, has been attempted before. The author rightly stresses that his aim is not to provide ready-made sermonettes for idle ministers, but rather seed thoughts that ministers may develop in their own way. As one who has never found the preparation of such talks easy, I believe I would have been greatly helped had I had such a book to hand.

These sermonettes have been written to introduce the sacrament of Baptism. They are addressed not only to the parents and the congregation, but often take the place of the customary children's address. They display a remarkable variety, and a selection is provided for Baptisms falling on the Christian festivals and other special occasions.

Those of us who are responsible for leading our people's worship should strive to make Baptism a memorable event, and yet how many of us use the occasion as an excuse to omit the usual sermonette for children? If we accept our reformed tradition, finely expressed in Robert Bruce's words at the beginning of the book, that Word and Sacrament are necessarily complementary, there can be no excuse for the omission. If we believe Baptism is once and for all, it is of great importance that Church members should be repeatedly reminded of its significance, and instructed in the many aspects of its meaning. I believe this book, if rightly used, may help to promote among our members that sense of exultation that encouraged Martin Luther. When in moments of doubt and depression he was wont to exclaim: '*Baptizatus sum*' – 'I have been baptized!'

PREFACE

I have gathered these talks together in the hope that ministers may find the material of use, not to preach verbatim but to remould according to their own circumstances. I would also hope that it might be of use to those ministers of other denominations who, while rejecting infant Baptism, hold services of infant dedication.

In practice, the talks were often abbreviated. When the parents are ill at ease, or the baby fractious, the preacher must temper his remarks accordingly.

The subject of infant Baptism raises theological questions and matters of controversy into which I shall not enter. I should, however, state the assumption which underlies these talks. Namely, that when Jesus blessed the little children it was no empty gesture, but a real blessing. His blessing given today can be no less real.

What happens in a Baptism then, though ineffable and inexplicable, is more than sign and symbol. It is – and this is what makes it a sacrament – an invisible work of the Spirit Who, as the rite is faithfully performed, passes into human lives even before those lives are capable of awareness. It is a meeting of Christ and the soul, and the sowing of the seed of our true life. Whether the seed will germinate and come to fruition, however, will depend on subsequent faith.

I have said these things in the talks that follow in as many different ways as possible; and I have tried to relate the talks to particular occasions. These vary, not only Sunday by Sunday, but also from parent to parent. For some parents it will be the first Baptism, for others the third or fourth; some will be more, others less attached to the congregation; some in the sometimes delicate situation of a mixed marriage, or a single parent family; one briefly home from abroad, another on the eve of departure – and so on. We should be sensitive to these things.

I address the congregation as well as the parents. Not only because words mumbled to the parents frustrate a congregation straining to hear them, but for the better reason that, in our Scottish tradition, the congregation are the godparents and their care for the families should be real.

The talks are less didactic than evangelical, for instruction has already been given in private. At the private interview I explain the sacrament along the lines of the statement from an Assembly Report which appears on a previous page. I also present the vows as a *sine qua non.*

Basically there are two vows: a profession of faith and a promise. They have recently been rephrased into more than two questions. My own preference, however, is for (1) a clear expression of faith in the Trinity: '*Do you confess your faith in God as your heavenly Father, in Jesus Christ as your Saviour and Lord, and in the Holy Spirit as your Helper?*' and (2) a promise which includes Christian nurture and example, and the completion of Baptism in communicant membership. Nowhere have I found this expressed with more clarity and directness than in the Order of the Church of South India whose phrases I have collated into a single question: '*Do you promise by God's help to provide a Christian home for this child; to bring him up in the ways of the Church of God; so to order your own lives that you do not cause this little one to stumble; and to encourage him later to be received into the full fellowship of the Church?*'

The first vow is generally understood; but should any admit difficulty with the Trinity I find Dr George

MacLeod's simple definition: 'God here, there and everywhere' (the Trinity in reverse) an excellent lead-in.

The second vow affords scope not only for instruction in private but for much of the teaching and, I hope, challenge incorporated in these talks.

Finally, I should explain that my normal procedure is to place the sacrament at the beginning of morning worship. *The Book of Common Order* (1979) declares that 'It is assumed that the Administration of Holy Baptism normally follows the Preaching of the Word.' When the sacrament precedes the main sermon, therefore, it is all the more necessary that this rubric be fulfilled by the giving of a brief talk: a practice which I find preferable to the far more difficult one of attempting to relate the main sermon (perhaps as often as once a month) to the Baptism which is to follow. When the Baptism is at the end of the service, a separate baptismal talk may of course be given; but for reasons psychological, practical and spiritual I choose to begin with the sacrament.

Part One

FOR ANY SUNDAY

Upside Down?

Here's a strange verse. 'Before they call, says the Lord, I will answer, and while they are yet speaking I will hear.'

It sounds upside down. 'Before they call, I will answer.' But a parent should get the point. You anticipate your baby's needs, you don't wait till your child tells you. You know already what he wants. You are there, on the spot when he needs you. Before he calls, you answer.

God is like that. He anticipates our needs. Not a sparrow falls to the ground but He is already there. That is what Baptism is about. Before your children know God, or have heard of Him, He is waiting here for them. Later on we pray that they will come to love Him. But, as the New Testament says, 'We love Him because He first loved us.'

And so today before they know their need of Baptism, almost before they know anything, God answers their need.

He answers their need to belong to His family, for only in this family can we find our true life and peace.

He answers their need for forgiveness. These babies haven't yet sinned, but when they do, one day, the gift of forgiveness and of cleansing will be there. Even before we sin, you see, He made provision for our sins; long ago He dealt with them and gave us pardon, on the Cross.

Your children will need the blessing, the help and the Spirit of God at all times, and they will be there. For you, too, they will be there. We need Him all the time if we are to live as His people. As the hymn says:

'Come, give us still Thy powerful aid,
And urge us on, and keep us Thine;
Nor leave the hearts that once were made
Fit temples for Thy grace divine.'

So it is that 'Before they call I will answer, and while they are yet speaking I will hear.'

Unconscious Recipients

There's a verse in the 127th Psalm which says, 'He giveth to his beloved in sleep.' The Jerusalem Bible translates it, 'He provides for his beloved as they sleep.'

The idea is that when our minds and bodies lie dormant, God is still at work. Deep in our unconscious lives His Spirit can be active.

It's a wonderful thought, that even when we have no awareness that He is there, God is often blessing us.

So also does He bless our children. These babies are quite unaware of any blessing coming to them today. Their minds and personalities are still dormant; their souls as if they were asleep. But 'He provides for his beloved as they sleep.' And they *are* His beloved, His jewels, His own.

One day, please God, your children will by a conscious act of faith join Christ's Church. Today they are the unconscious recipients of His grace. The gifts of God, this reminds us, are not something we earn, or have consciously to strive for, but something we receive.

You have brought Jennifer and Morag here to receive His blessing and His Spirit, and all the welcome and the promise that are in this lovely sacrament. Will you continue to bring them to Him often, at home and later through Church and Sunday School, until they find themselves coming to Him eagerly and naturally, of their own free choice.

An Unbreakable Bond

What a marvellous sacrament this is. It means that because you, the parents, have come here as Christians, bringing your children to Christ, they belong to Him too. 'The promise is to you and your children.'

That does not mean that some day they won't need conversion. The gift of God given today may live in them unused, and we, along with you, must work and pray that they may use it. I suppose this is what an old minister meant when he prayed, 'May this child be so baptized that he may never need to be converted.' He meant, may the blessing given in Baptism ever increase; may it be like that 'light that shines more and more to the perfect day.' And this can surely happen.

But the first step is simply that God bestows sonship on them, calls them His own. They were born Adam's children, part of the human race. Today they become heirs of the second Adam, heirs of Christ, and children of His. And this can never be undone.

Think of the prodigal son. Through no merit of his own he was the son of a good father. He despised his sonship and abused it. It didn't mean a thing to him. Yet one day he could say the word 'father': 'I will return to my father.' He was still in that relationship.

A relationship is established today between God and your children which nothing can break. Its establishing never needs to be repeated. It is a given fact: it is there. God makes a covenant with your children today that will never be broken, neither by sin nor death.

We can only wonder at this, at the faithfulness of God, and praise His name.

Passport to Glory

Today I shall just preface the Baptism with some words of an old King of France – Louis IX, who became St Louis. This is what he said:

'I think more of the place where I was baptized than of the Cathedral of Rheims where I was crowned; for the dignity of a child of God which was bestowed on me at baptism is greater than that of a ruler of a kingdom. The latter I shall lose at death, the other shall be my passport to everlasting glory.'

That's worth repeating, isn't it? Here it is again…

Receiving (1)

How do we know God? And how can our children know Him?

Charles Wesley, in one of his hymns, tells us. He says:

> 'God through Himself we then shall know
> If Thou within us shine.'

By 'Thou' he means the Holy Spirit. As we receive the Spirit of God we know God. Not by wondering if there is a God, or searching for Him. But He comes to us, seeks us, dwells in us.

Baptism is God coming to a child even before the child can know He has come.

You have brought John, and you wait with him before God. But you cannot baptize him, and I cannot baptize him. It is the Holy Spirit who baptizes him.

That is why you bring him now, when he is so helpless.

He can't initiate anything. He can't give. He can only receive.

And we have to go on receiving the Holy Spirit all our lives; that is what being a Christian is. Not trying to live a good life, but receiving new life from God.

Whether your children will do this depends above all on the example of their parents. They will learn to kneel as you kneel; to worship as you worship.

May you, and your children, and especially John, receive what the Holy Spirit would give you, today and always.

Receiving (2)

Jesus once took a basin of water and washed His disciples' feet. He was teaching them to serve one another and to be willing to do the kind of service that has no glamour, that is just a chore.

But there was more to it than that. When He came to Peter and Peter refused to have his feet washed, Jesus told him he must. He must let Jesus do this to him: it was terribly important. Why? Because serving and giving are not the only things: there has to be receiving as well. Peter had to receive what Jesus wanted to give him; and that meant not just the washing of his feet but, as Jesus said, a spiritual cleansing.

Here, too, today we are to receive what Jesus gives. One of the great points about a baby's Baptism is that the baby doesn't do anything. He can't give, he can only receive. (I believe some people, talking about it, say, I've had the child *done*, or, Is the child *done*?)

Yes, he can receive. Jesus would not have taken the children in His arms and blessed them, if they could not receive a blessing.

So the Christian life begins in an act of receiving. The child receives the water, which stands for the cleansing grace of God; and all through his life, if he is to be a Christian he will turn to Jesus, turn to God, and receive. This is what it's all about: what we are here on earth for. To serve God, yes, and to glorify Him: but we can only do that as we are open to Him, and receive Him.

As we come to the sacrament let us ask that not only James but his parents, and not only this family but the whole family of this congregation, may receive what God is waiting to bestow; and go out afterwards with Christ's joy and peace in all our hearts.

Water Pure and Tranquil

Someone described a little child at rest as 'like tranquil water reflecting Heaven'. We older folk can't reflect heaven like that. The clear water has been polluted by the world. The new-born child has in him the seeds of both good and evil but he is, to begin with, unspoiled. He has done no deliberate acts of wrong. He is, it has also been said, 'fenced off from the world and guarded by angels.'

Gradually, God will withdraw those angels and leave you, the parents, to take their place. Your task is to see not only to their physical wellbeing, but that the image of heaven in them, though never so clear as now, is never lost. May they always be as pure water flowing into a widening loch.

The importance of Baptism is this: that it is the opening of their lives to Jesus Christ, for His grace to come to them. May that precious stream never, by any fault or negligence of ours, be dammed up. May He who today will begin a good work in your children be permitted to continue it, according to His loving purpose, until they are established and confirmed as His disciples.

That at life's end the water may again be tranquil, reflecting heaven.

What Makes a Home?

A crossword puzzle had the clue 'It makes a home', and there were nine letters. Someone suggested 'furniture' but that didn't fit. Eventually they got it. A-F-F-E-C-T-I-O-N.

And that's the truth, or, at any rate, a vital part of it. It is not bricks and mortar or any material possessions that make a home. It is not even the fact that it is your own place, and you have the keys. It is the atmosphere created there. The affection, yes, but also the loyalty and trust, the courtesy and respect, and all the sharing and forgiving and encouraging that goes on in the family: these things make a home. A place where parents show understanding and give gentle guidance, and where children are thoughtful as well as loving towards their parents.

You will be asked today, Will you provide a Christian home for your children? That's a big creative task, when you think about it. But Jesus said, 'Seek first the kingdom of God, and all these things will be given unto you'; and this is one of the things that are given, that come spontaneously when the people involved are seeking first the kingdom of God.

In other words, if you have the right priorities, your home (and indeed your whole life) will sort itself out.

Coming here today to have Kenneth and Glenda baptized is a right priority. Bringing them, and bringing yourselves to Christ; asking for and receiving His blessing; acknowledging your children's need of him, now and all through their lives; declaring your vows and taking your place with all who accept Him and love Him here in His Church: these are all the right priorities.

It was into a loving home, and a home in which God's

name was treasured, that God entrusted His Son. It was through the influence of His earthly parents, through their example, through sharing in that home at Nazareth for thirty years, and through accepting His own part of the responsibility there – even by becoming the chief breadwinner when Joseph died – it was by all this that Jesus grew in grace and in wisdom. May your home and your children be strengthened today as we come in faith to God and accept all that He would bestow in Jesus Christ our Lord.

A New Relationship

There is a great moment in the Book of the Revelation when St John, in his vision, sees Jesus sitting on His throne; and Jesus is saying, 'Behold, I make all things new.'

Is not this the meaning of Baptism? In Baptism God takes the life of a child (or it may be of a man or woman) and places it on a new foundation. When we are born we have a relationship with our parents and with God our Heavenly Father. But in Baptism there is something new: we are brought into a relationship with Jesus Christ.

The central fact about Baptism is this communion with Christ – and when we bring the children to Him He takes them in His arms and makes them His own.

I would like to read you this morning a paragraph from the Report of the Commission on Baptism which our Church set up a few years ago. 'The act of Christ in Baptism', it says, 'is one which avails for the whole of our life, and reaches out beyond into the resurrection and the new creation. Therefore in Baptism we are united to Christ as members of His Body in a relationship in which we are made to grow in union with Him as we feed on Him through faith by the power of His Word and Spirit, and find our help not in ourselves but wholly in Him.'

In His Hands

Jesus took the little ones in His arms and blessed them. What difference did it make? What happened to these babies afterwards? Nothing special. I suspect they grew up, like anyone else, to be tradesmen, or wives and mothers, or fishermen, or farmers. And some, I'm afraid, would become prodigal sons.

Perhaps, though, one or two mothers remembered that Jesus had blessed their children that day: and because they saw Him as a man of God, it had brought home to them that God loved and cared for, and welcomed, their children.

And this is what Baptism means. It's a rough world, and we all have our share of sorrow, suffering, temptation, injustice – some more than others. But we are still, as the hymn says, 'safe in the arms of Jesus', and in the hands of God.

'He's got the whole world in His hands'. It might not look like it, but it is so. No powers of evil will ever capture the world, take it from God. As St Paul says, whatever happens (and he lists the calamities) 'who shall separate us from the love of God?'

The negroes in slavery knew that they were at the same time in God's hands. 'He's got the whole world', they sang. 'He's got you and me brother ... He's got the little bitsy baby ... the Church ... the whole world, in His hands.'

He's got your little bitsy baby in His hands. Today Jesus takes her in His arms. Then she is given back into your arms. And you are asked to vow to care for her as a child of God, and to see that she grows to know Him.

We will bring all the love, the teaching and the support of the Church to help you to fulfil your task.

Dying to Live

The word 'baptize' comes from the Greek word *baptizein* which means 'to dip'. All the first Christians, adults and children together, were baptized by immersion. They were not just sprinkled but went down under the water – as the Baptists and others still do. Sprinkling signifies cleansing and the fact that Christ washes away our sins, and we need that profoundly. But we should never forget what immersion symbolizes so vividly: death and resurrection.

You go down under the water as if leaving the old life; you come up again to begin life anew. Well, that is certainly meaningful in regard to an adult, but is it meaningful in the life of a child? Yes, because it says something not only about adults but about human nature. It says that we must, in a spiritual sense, die to belong to God.

By nature, right from our birth, we are self-centred, not God-centred. We are self-willing, self-seeking, self-glorifying. And, if our lives are to be lived to the glory of God, all that has to die.

St Paul says somewhere that we are 'baptized into the death of Christ.' That must mean that we are to share in His death. How? Well, his death wasn't just a martyrdom, the putting to death of a good man. It was an offering, a giving up of Himself to God for our sakes. To be baptized into His death is to offer up ourselves to God, to give up our self-concern, as the hymn says 'to pour contempt on all our pride.' That is not something we achieve once and for all at Baptism. We have, as St Paul says, to die daily.

That is something your children will have to learn; for

in spite of their being baptized today, the old Adam will keep cropping up, and asserting himself in them. But in Baptism we see that God loves them, that Christ died for them, and that even now, at the beginning of their lives, He is claiming them and telling them they are children of God. Let them know some day that through faith in Him who came to them even before they had any faith, they can live not unto themselves but to His glory.

Whom is He Like?

'Who is baby like?' That's what everyone asks. Is he like his father or his mother, his grandad or even his uncles: and which of his big brothers or sisters is he like?

Today we look, and we see another family resemblance. He is like God, his Father – because we are all made in the image of God. He has stamped His own likeness on the human soul, with its capacity for hope and love, forgiveness and generosity, tenderness and courage, holiness and truth.

One day the Scribes came to Jesus with a question. 'Should we pay tax to Caesar?' 'Show me a coin', He said. 'Whose image is on it?' 'Caesar's.' 'Then render Caesar the things that are Caesar's, and God the things that are God's.'

Today we render William unto God because God's image is stamped on him; he comes from God, belongs to God, and will one day return to God.

As we render him, God will accept and bless him in this lovely sacrament. And I will sprinkle water on his head in the sign of a cross, to signify that he belongs not only to God, but also to Christ who died for him and for us all, and who claims us for His own.

For William, let us pray that the image of God and of Jesus Christ may be so evident in his life that one day men seeing him may come to glorify God his Father.

Jesus Loves Me

'Jesus loves me, this I know
For the Bible tells me so,
Little ones to Him belong,
They are weak, but He is strong.'

I suppose this, and 'Away in a manger' will be the first two hymns Graham will learn. The first one, 'Jesus loves me', is really what Baptism is all about.

First it says 'Jesus loves me' – and that means that God loves me, for Jesus mirrors God. God doesn't just love us all, but *me*. That's why, when Graham is baptized, I say his name. The Good Shepherd knows each sheep by name, and His love reaches out today to Graham, and also to you.

How do we know God loves us like this? 'For the Bible tells me so'. Not so many children are brought up on the Bible now. Well, then, 'For my mother tells me so'. All the more reason for her doing that. And remember what St Augustine said: 'I would not be Your child, O God, if You had not given me such a mother.'

And why not, 'For my father tells me so'? Too many fathers opt out. But a boy will often take it from his dad, listen to what Dad has to say, accept or reject Christ's claims as his dad accepts or rejects them.

John Baillie, a great Scottish churchman and teacher, said that he learned to respect and obey his parents because he saw that they were under authority too – to Someone higher than themselves – to God. He came to God through them.

'Little ones to Him belong'. Baptism is about belonging. Being brought into the fellowship of the Church, into this great family of God. In the Church we acknowledge that together we belong to God. 'All souls are mine, says the Lord.'

'They are weak, but He is strong'. Not only physically weak, but too weak, as human beings, to go it alone. Baptism speaks of forgiveness and renewal and grace, which all men need.

May His Spirit be with you today in your home, and may you and Graham remain in His family, where His grace is to be found.

He Calls Them by Name

I shall be preaching today about the parables of the lost coin, the lost sheep, and the lost (or prodigal) son.

If there is one message underlying all these parables it is the particular, individual love of God. He calls His sheep by name and every one of them matters.

The same message is in this sacrament. The minister pronounces the child's name not to give her the name – you have done that already – but because her name denotes that she isn't just any baby but an individual, different from any other and especially dear, as each one of us is especially dear, to God.

You are now the parents of two children, and you will find that you love each of them especially in his, or her, own way. You love them equally and infinitely, but differently. So also does God.

As Rosemary grows she will become herself more and more, and come to God in her own way, and make her own response to Him. Your task is to help Him in this new creation. Not to impose your own pattern on her, but to give God the opportunities to fashion her according to His own pattern. To surround her with such prayers and love that she will awake naturally towards Him, that she will pass easily from her trust in you to a trust in Him whom you trust.

Beneficiaries by Faith

I once asked a non-churchgoer if he had been baptized. 'Yes', he said, 'but I never asked to be.' He thought it unfair that anyone should choose the Christian way of life, and Christian belief, for him without his consent.

Well, you are choosing the Christian life for your children. You are claiming God's promises for them by faith. You don't want them to miss the benefits of this sacrament; benefits that will come to them in response to your faith and the Church's faith and, later on, their own faith.

We all want to give our children the best in life. One of the best things of all is that we are members of Christ's Church. We want them to share in that too, even when they are too young to choose it for themselves.

My friend said he had never asked to be baptized. Neither had he asked to be born as a Scot, which most of us would regard as a boon. He never asked to be born into a good and loving home, or to be given certain talents which he undoubtedly possesses. There are so many things we are given that we don't ask for, and it is not unfair because we are free, as life goes on, to deny, or reject or misuse them. But it is far better to pray the prayer, 'Lord we live by your bounty: may we live to Your glory.'

The very life of God is given us in the sacraments. But many of us have received His free bounty in another way – through our parents. To young children God is mediated through godly parents. They may worship their mother and have implicit faith in their father. Alter two words in the hymn, and it is still true:

'Jesus loves me, this I know
For my mother tells me so.'

Before they can understand the Bible, the word of God can reach them at their mother's knee.

I am reminded of the Chinese woman who, when she was an exile, learned to read. She then wrote this prayer: 'We are going home to many who cannot read. So, Lord, make us to be Bibles, so that those who cannot read the Book can read it in us.'

When your children grow older, your lives will still speak to them. 'The way he himself lived', wrote one man of his father, 'and the kind of being he was, exercised over me a more profound and lasting constraint than all his spoken words of command.'

So, let the strength of Christ lead you in your living and let your light so shine before your children that they may come to glorify their Father who is in heaven.

Nurture

A friend of mine, who is a minister, called on a nursery-gardener in his congregation. He was shown some marvellous chrysanthemums, and he said, 'I've never seen any like these; how do you grow them?' 'Well', said the gardener, 'you should know. They are the same plants I sold you in the early summer.'

The same plants hadn't produced the same results in the manse garden. Why not? The gardener gave the answer in one word – 'nurture.' He had nurtured his plants in every possible way: seen to the soil, the fertilizer, the disbudding, the watering; and he got the results.

It's the same with a human life. The second question at a Baptism used to be 'Do you promise to bring him up in the nurture and admonition of the Lord?' Now it is usually spelled out in simpler language, because a phrase like 'nurture and admonition' doesn't cut home today.

All the same 'nurture' is a fine word. It means, of course, to nourish. Most parents cherish their children but not so many nourish them, not in the sense of 'the nurture of the Lord'. Many parents, frankly, don't know how to do it: how to foster the love of God and of Jesus, and to help their children to grow into the beauty and wholeness of a Christian life.

But God knows our need, and He has given His church to help us. On the certificate I will give you is written: 'Baptized in the name of the Father, and of the Son and of the Holy Spirit *and brought into the fellowship of the Church.*'

Here there is nurture. Those who try to live as Christians without the fellowship of the Church are deprived of the rich soil of faith and knowledge, of grace and inspiration, that are here.

May baby Jean, and also her brothers and sisters, and you their parents, be so thirled to the Church that you will find all the help you need to your lives' end.

May we, who also are the Church, be true godparents. (You have made it clear by carrying your own baby that we, and no-one else, are the godparents.) May we provide the nurture of a live and concerned congregation, a truly Christian soil in which young lives may grow.

The Church's One Foundation

We have sung 'The Church's one foundation'. That hymn of four verses says four things about the Church; and they are all worth underlining at a Baptism.

Verse 1: 'She is his new creation
By water and the word.'

From the beginning the apostles went out preaching the gospel, baptizing those who believed, and forming them into congregations. People were recreated, became a new kind of men and women, and were bound together in a new fellowship.

That's how the Church grows still. The gospel is proclaimed, men are recreated by Christ and enter the fellowship by Baptism, and they bring their children that they too may hear the Gospel as they grow, and respond and become Christ's new creation.

Verse 2: 'Elect from every nation,
Yet one o'er all the earth.'

Christ's people form one great worldwide family, elect, that is called out from the rest of mankind. A distinct people. At the General Election, shortly, men and women will be elected, called out, to serve as MPs. In Baptism Brian is called out, selected or elected, to serve Jesus Christ. As we all are, by virtue of our Baptism. And just as he is a Paterson and differentiated from all those not of the Paterson family, so he is different, by Baptism, from those who do not hold or practise the Christian faith, or belong to the Christian fellowship, or have the Christian's relationship with Jesus Christ.

Verse 3 speaks of the Church waiting for peace:
'Till with the vision glorious,
Her longing eyes are blest.'

Those identified with the Church through Baptism share in a great vision. In a troubled world the Church is the guardian of a great hope. God's kingdom will come, His will be done. May Brian grow up to share this vision.

Verse 4: 'Yet she on earth hath union,
With God the Three in One.'

The Church links earth and heaven. Through the Church we are in touch with the eternal. Through the gospel, through Christian worship, fellowship and work, and through the sacraments, the heavens are opened and we know we belong to two worlds. May Brian grow up not just in one world, but in two; may the God who blesses him today be known to him, and to you his parents always.

The Divine Wooing

Suppose you were given charge of a child not your own: a child who had no feeling for you, to whom you were a stranger. What would you do?

Try to win his confidence, of course. He couldn't trust you just because he was told he had to. You would have to *create* faith in him. And you would have to set about it gently, with words and gestures, smiles and perhaps gifts, in order to convey the kindness you felt. Gradually, you would put him at ease, and of his own free will he would come to you.

With ourselves and God it is not exactly like that, because we are already His children. Yet He is a stranger to us to begin with, and He has to woo us and win us. The sacrament of Baptism is not His first advance towards us. What lies behind it is the fact that He sent Jesus to live and to die for us, and to draw us to Himself. Then God comes to us in our parents' love, which makes us ready to accept His love. (But how difficult it is for a child from a loveless home to think of God as a Father.)

Baptism is not the first approach: but through it God is speaking to your child, not in words – he's too young for words – but through the gentle and loving presence of Jesus. Later on, through the Bible and Church, through the works and words of Jesus, and through the living Spirit of Jesus in men and women, God will make other advances to your son. Then, please God, Andrew will come to Him of his own free will, to be His loving disciple to his life's end.

His Praise Shall Sound

We have sung a hymn full of joy at God's creation.

> 'From all that dwell below the skies,
> Let the Creator's praise arise'.

At Harvest Festival we rejoice in His creation in nature: and at a Baptism in His creation of man.

Jesus spoke of the joy of human creation. 'A woman in childbirth suffers', He said, 'because her time has come; but when she has given birth to the child she forgets the suffering in her joy that a man has been born into the world.'

The joy of creation! But creation is not enough. We are born unfinished: we still need redemption. We are born to be born again. That is why Christ came, and why He died.

So the hymn goes on:

> 'Let the Redeemer's name be sung,
> Through every land in every tongue'.

This is the meaning of the water, the meaning of the Cross, the purpose of being 'ingrafted into Christ'.

Remember, too, how the hymn ends:

> 'Thy praise shall sound from shore to shore,
> Till suns shall rise and set no more'.

That is the ultimate purpose of our lives – that we should sound forth God's praise. Not just that your baby, as he grows, should be a credit to you: but that his life should join with others, the world over, who are sounding the praise of God.

A Christian Heritage

When St Paul wrote to his young friend, Timothy, he said this: 'I am reminded of the sincerity of your faith, a faith which was alive in Lois your grandmother and Eunice your mother before you.'

We see there how faith can be handed down, not by any magic, not automatically, but by a child growing up in a gracious Christian home.

I am reminded of the tribute that Dr D.S. Cairns, a great Scottish churchman of my boyhood, paid to his father. 'Here', he wrote, 'from my earliest childhood had been one beside me influencing me in a thousand gentle ways in favour of uprightness, kindness, unselfishness and faith, making it easier at every stage for me to believe in goodness and in God. God Himself had all my life through my father been telling me how He felt towards me and how He would have me think and act.'

General Osborne of the Salvation Army, in his autobiography, has said the same about his mother. 'Long before I knew of God in Christ', he says, 'I saw Him and loved Him in my mother.'

Well, then, like all good parents you want to give your children the best chance in life. A good education, worthwhile interests, decent friends, holidays to remember, and many other things. But the best thing of all is what St Paul's young friend Timothy had: a family tradition of faith, and a living spiritual example in each generation.

May it be like that with you and your children; and may this sacrament bring you, with them, to the feet of Christ.

A New Song

(*After Psalm 96*) 'O sing a new song to the Lord' – you will have a new song in your hearts today. A song of joy, and of love (more love than you had before) and of gratitude to God.

I think today of that new song called 'The Magnificat' which Mary sang when she knew her child, God's Son, was to be born: 'My soul doth magnify the Lord and my spirit hath rejoiced in God my Saviour. For He hath regarded the low estate of His handmaiden.'

It was a humble song: and you must feel humble today at being entrusted with a child. You must be asking yourselves, how can we, who are so inadequate, especially in things spiritual, bring him up in the ways of God? Well, you will find that both Church and day-school will help (especially, I hope, the Church, for we are the godparents). Above all, there's just the atmosphere of your home. When Jesus prayed for His disciples He said, 'For their sakes I sanctify myself', and parents creating a home for their children can pray that too: 'For their sakes I sanctify myself.' Or, remember the words of Joshua's vow, the vow of a parent, 'As for me and my house, we will serve the Lord.'

As well as being a humble song, Mary's new song was one of rejoicing. She rejoiced in the good news of the coming salvation. When I sprinkle the water on your child today we are remembering, and celebrating, the good news that Jesus saves, that He makes us clean. So, as well as rejoicing at the gift of a child, we rejoice at His gift of salvation, of Himself, that is, as our Saviour: the gift that every child, and every man and woman, needs.

Responding to the Gospel

Someone once described a sacrament as *verbum visibile* – the Word (or the gospel) made visible. Baptism is certainly the gospel made visible, for the gospel is the good news that God loves us. Today we see clearly that He loves us before we love Him, and before we can do anything about it.

You don't say to your children, 'Be good, and then I'll start loving you.' Neither does God. Love comes first, both with us and with Him. 'We love Him', the Bible says, 'because He first loved us.' And this is the gospel – the pure, undeserved love of God.

What can *we* do? We can only respond. As you have responded to the love that is in this sacrament, to the Spirit of Christ in the sacrament, by bringing your children today. We grown-ups can also respond by what we do with our lives; for as the hymn says:

> 'Love so amazing, so divine,
> Demands my soul, my life, my all.'

It isn't so easy for your children to respond when they start to grow. It is especially difficult for boys. How many boys over the age of ten, for instance, will come here, to church, on their own? They only come when their parents come. One reason, of course, is the influence of other boys; away from their family they don't like to be different.

So a great deal depends on the parents, later on. That's why I would urge you, as you take your vows, to make the resolve once made by Joshua when he said, 'As for me and my house, we will serve the Lord.'

A Startling Saying

When Jesus set a child in the midst and said 'Of such is the Kingdom of Heaven', He was saying one of the most startling and original things ever said.

It doesn't seem all that startling to us, two thousand years later. Because we have come to worship children, or at any rate to yield to their charms. It wasn't always like that, however. Two thousand years ago few people would have taken seriously the suggestion that a child is higher or holier than a man. 'It would have seemed', said G.K. Chesterton, 'like the suggestion that a tadpole is higher or holier than a frog...It would sound like saying that a bud must be more beautiful than a flower or that an unripe apple must be better than a ripe one.'

Why then is there, to us, something infinitely precious in a child?

Because in His own coming as a child Jesus exalted all childhood.

Because He loved children, and loves them still.

Because they are made for God and from the day of their birth their destiny is Heaven.

And because now, the time of childhood, is the time of their innocence. Later on they will gain in wisdom and knowledge and in many things; but they will lose something by the slow corruption of the world. Unless, of course, they move through the world in company with Christ: and that is what we wish for this child today. It is what we pray for him, as we bring him to Christ for Baptism; and it is what we ask his parents to give him through their own Christian love and example.

The Vocation of Parenthood

One of the features of life today is the number of people who have no sense of vocation, no mission in life. It isn't always their own fault. Many feel they are misfits, and that the work they do – the only work open to them, perhaps – does not call out the best they have to give.

But anyone who is a parent is largely delivered from that sense of frustration. I sometimes say to couples whom I am preparing for marriage, If you become good parents, no matter what else goes wrong – if you lose your job, or never get to the top or make much money – that doesn't matter. You are not a failure. To be a successful father or mother is to have done the most worthwhile thing of all.

Here, in parenthood, is a great mission in life. Here in your child is someone to serve, someone to live at your best for.

You are going to pledge yourselves by prayer, precept and example to bring Janet up in the Christian way of life. And that involves the dedication of yourselves.

A Prime Minister, called to office, was surrounded by newspapermen who congratulated him. 'I don't need your congratulations', he said, 'but I need your prayers.' Amid all the congratulations you have received, and the good wishes, remember that you are also surrounded by our prayers. The Church constantly prays for its parents and children, and from now on you are included.

In a way your coming here today is an act of prayer, of thanksgiving and of supplication. And because God is the Hearer and Answerer of prayer, He will bless you, and Janet today, even above all that you ask or think.

Partings

Tonight we will be commissioning a missionary before she sets out for India. It will be inspiring to see a young person give herself to God, and be given the Church's blessing as she goes to serve Christ in a strange land. But there will also be a sadness, especially for her parents whom she is not to see again for three years. And she has a great friend whom she may not see for an even longer period, because her friend is going to Africa and their furloughs will not coincide.

This is what often happens to human relationships, the sadness of partings. It happens most often in the relationship of parent and child. On the other hand, we must not forget that these parents are giving their daughter willingly and even gladly to the service of Christ in India. To give up a child willingly is a very great thing.

At this Baptism children and parents are united in Jesus Christ. And your hope is that for as long as possible you may remain united. Eventually your children must grow up and leave home, but you hope they will always be near you and in close contact.

But, you know, the only way we can really keep our children is by sowing the love of Christ in their hearts, and by loving Him ourselves. And for those who love one another in Jesus Christ there is no real parting, not ever, not to all eternity.

Today, in Baptism, is the beginning of such a relationship. The seed is sown today. May it be so nurtured that whether, in days to come, you and your children be together or apart, nothing will ever separate you, because you are in God's hands, and held in the love of Jesus Christ our Lord.

Not Potters but Gardeners

Dr Crichton-Miller, a well-known psychologist, used to say this to parents: 'You are not potters to mould clay, but gardeners to protect bulbs.'

You see what he means. Your child's life is not to be entirely shaped by you. He has a life of his own, which God has given him. He must realize himself, and develop in the way God means him to develop.

But, on the other hand, he needs protection. As a young bulb needs protection from the poisons in the soil, and from the severity of the climate.

We can see that the soil of our homes is not poisoned by lovelessness or antagonisms, by selfishness or greed. But what of the climate, the climate of the world? It is made by the beliefs and behaviour of grown men and women. We talk of the political climate and of the climate of opinion and of morals fostered by the mass media. But the politicians and broadcasters and newsmen are just people, like ourselves. The climate is made by the values we and they accept, the lives we and they live.

For the sake of our children we must improve the world's climate; and we must, in the language of the Bible, sanctify ourselves. That is why parents are asked to take vows. Because your home is to be part of that garden, as this church is another part of it, in which the young bulbs can safely grow.

As you take your vows today, can I remind you of the vows taken long ago by Joshua as an example to the whole people. 'As for me and my house', he said, 'we will serve the Lord.' That's the best vow of all.

Tell Me Who I Am

There was a strange event in World War I. After a shambles of a battle a soldier was found wandering about in a daze. He had lost his memory. He didn't know who he was, and his jacket and identification disc were missing.

The colonel to whom he was brought tried to identify him before sending him to the base hospital, but with no success.

After a few days the battalion, now resting, got up a boxing tournament. The lad was taken into the ring, and the colonel said, 'Can anyone tell me who he is?' And some of his mates claimed him.

In a way, that soldier asking, 'Can anyone tell me who I am?' stands for everyone born into the world. Because this is the most basic of all questions. Can anyone tell us who we are, apart from being human beings? Does anyone claim us, and give us an identity, and a reason for being here on earth?

Well, this is what Baptism is about. About God claiming us and saying, You belong to me; you are a child of mine.

As we baptize this child today we are telling him who he is and to whom he belongs. To his parents, yes certainly, entrusted to their love and care. But also, and even more significantly, to God, who sent His Son, Jesus, to tell us who we are and to claim us.

As you acknowledge this claim now and turn to Him, He comes to your little one and says, Let him come to me, for of such is my kingdom. And He blesses him, and gives him not his Christian name (you have given him that already) but his identity as a beloved child of God.

Latent Powers

We have a good organist, and we are very fortunate. But he would be the first to tell you that it was a master organist who gave a recital here the other night. The organist of St Giles' Cathedral showed us the full capabilities of our organ; not only its power but every gradation of expression that is in it.

It strikes me that every human life is like an organ waiting for the master organist to show what is in it.

Your hopes for your children are that they might realize themselves to the full. You yourselves want to bring out the best in them.

In many lives there are latent powers, which are never set free: powers of love and tenderness, of unselfishness, and of friendship. Powers of personality, yes, and of spirituality.

Only when our lives are touched by the Master, by Jesus Christ, can they become fully alive. That's why a certain old minister used to say at every Baptism, 'I baptize thee in the Name of the Father, and of the Son, and of the Holy Ghost, and I claim thee for Christ my Master.'

You have brought them here today that He may lay His hands on them and bless them. That is the beginning. We pray that His Spirit may be ever upon them; the Spirit that sets men free, that releases the hidden splendour, and makes us new creatures.

> 'I am come that they might have life, and have it more abundantly.'

Your children have been given the gift of life. May they be born again into that more abundant life that is in Jesus.

Promise and Fulfilment

The gladioli in my garden are beginning to thrust their spears through the soil, and I think of the lovely flowers that are to come. Those tiny spears are full of promise. I love them for themselves, but even more for what they will be in a few months' time.

You love your tiny mite of a boy for what he is, and also for the promise of what he may become.

Notice that I say 'may' not 'will' become. A child is even more delicate than a flower. We can so easily stand in his way and prevent the promise from being fulfilled.

The positive thing to remember is that a child needs very much the same things as a flower.

First, to be planted firmly and early in good soil. 'We must be planted if we are to grow', said a man of simple wisdom. Today at his Baptism God is planting your Tom firmly in the soil of His Church. Jesus said 'It is not the will of your Father that any of these little ones should perish', and that is why we are given the Church and its sacraments, as the rich soil in which we can take root and grow.

There is also, of course, the soil of a good home. Ask God to make your home one where affection is deep, and goodness and truth take root and grow; and where the qualities of Christian character will pass naturally from you to your children.

The second requirement for a flower is sunshine. For a child – well, 'Walk in the light', said Jesus. The best light your child can walk in is the radiance shed by Jesus Himself. So, let all the grace and love of Jesus shine on him always. Keep him in the rays of that true sun. And, in words you will hear again in this service, 'May the

Lord make His face to shine upon him: may He lift up His countenance upon him, and give him peace.'

A Word for Fathers

Though I am talking to all of you, I have a special word today for fathers: not that the fathers here today are different from any other fathers.

The role of the father, both in the family and at a Baptism, is often undervalued. Here is an extreme example. A woman came and asked me to baptize her baby. Having heard what she had to say I agreed, and fixed a date, and for some special reason it had to be on a weeknight. 'But', I said, 'we can't go ahead until I have seen your husband too; it is as much his affair as yours.' They both came back, and we went through the form of service and the meaning of the sacrament. Then came the day of the Baptism and she turned up with the baby, but no husband. 'Where's the father?' I asked. 'Oh', she said, 'he's outside holding the dog!'

They still thought that she was the only one that mattered. After all, was it not her job to bring up the children?

In contrast, listen to what St Paul says, in Ephesians, 'And ye fathers provoke not your children to wrath: but bring them up in the nurture and admonition of the Lord.'

Most of us would see it as a matter for both husband and wife, who are partners in parenthood. But it is interesting that it is the fathers that St Paul addresses himself to.

What is the charge he gives them? First, do not provoke your children. Other translations say, 'Do not over-correct them', or 'exasperate' or 'irritate' them. Certainly children can be exasperating, but don't give them cause. God is long-suffering with us, and we must be so too.

Second, bring them up in the nurture and admonition of the Lord. That used to be one of the vows at Baptism: 'Will you bring him up in the nurture and admonition of the Lord?' We express it now in more modern language. What St Paul meant is clearer in other translations. 'The discipline and instruction of the Lord', says one. 'Bring them up tenderly with true Christian training and advice', says another. And the New English Bible puts it this way: 'Give them the instruction and the correction which belong to a Christian upbringing.'

Well, that's all very important, and I'm afraid we fall down on it a lot. It isn't easy to give instruction and correction, and parents need to support each other in doing it.

But more important still is to do what you are doing today. To bring your children to Christ – and I emphasize the word *bring*. It is not enough, when the time comes, just to send them to Sunday School and to hope they will go to Church. You have to shepherd them; and, remember the shepherd, in Bible days, always led his sheep from in front. Set the example yourselves; open your own hearts to the grace of God; and may the same Christ who lays His Hands on your little ones today, bless you all in your homes through all the years to come.

A Covenant is Sealed

We baptize children 'in the Name of the Father, and of the Son, and of the Holy Spirit.' What does this mean?

It means that we baptize them not just into this congregation, but into the faith and fellowship of all Christian people.

Also, that I will be baptizing these two children not in, or into, the names of Fleming and McLean: but in the name of Jesus Christ. Because a relationship is to be established with Him.

It is quite possible, of course, for a child to grow up and forget he has been brought to Jesus at his baptism: to forget it, or to dismiss it as unimportant; or even to turn away from Christ.

It is quite possible for a child to grow up and deny his parenthood – yet the parenthood remains a fact. Whatever their future, nothing can take away what is done for your children today: the fact that a covenant is made, a transaction has taken place with Jesus Christ, who has set His seal on them in this sacrament.

May they never want to forget it. May they come to realize all they now are by Baptism. May the relationship with Jesus Christ, indeed with Father, Son and Holy Spirit, grow even stronger.

You, the parents, are to help them to realize it, and we, the congregation, will assist you. By your own faith, your own life and example, your own knowledge that you too were baptized in the name of the Father, the Son and the Holy Spirit, you can do it.

They are, the service says, 'engaged to confess the faith of Christ crucified.' An engagement is a promise, and it looks forward. We look forward to the day when, together with us all, they love and worship and serve the

Lord Jesus Christ and His Father through the power of the Holy Spirit.

Brought to Jesus

We read that 'they brought young children to Jesus'. They brought them: they could have sent them, the older ones anyway, but they didn't send them, they brought them. Perhaps they wanted to come themselves.

To bring your child – is not this the right way? You have brought him today. In five, ten or fifteen years what will you be doing? Bringing him, or sending him – or, as some parents do, not bothering. 'It's up to him: he can do as he likes.'

In bringing them today, you are acting for your children, making a decision for them that they can't yet make for themselves. I am not suggesting that you should always do that. Compulsion, especially in the matter of religion, is often counter-productive. But to bring without compulsion is the best way of all. To bring your children with you because you want to turn towards Jesus yourselves, and because through you they are drawn to Him – that is best.

'They brought young children' – where? Not to a place, not to a church, but 'to Jesus'. And a child needs Jesus. Many of us can't remember a time when we did not know and love the name of Jesus, because from our birth our parents had brought us to Him.

This sacrament speaks of Him, of His power and His love and His blessing. So you haven't just brought them to the church: you have brought them to Jesus. Because they need Him now, and they and we need Him all our days.

A True Man

What do you want for Peter as you bring him to his baptism? To see him grow up to be a true man. Surely that is your deepest longing.

So – what is a true man? 'What *is* man?' asked the Psalmist, but he didn't leave it there. 'What *is* man that Thou art mindful of him?' If you believe in a God who cares for us, who has spoken to us, all through history and especially through the coming of Jesus Christ, then you must also see that we are creatures with a special destiny: even with a glory and a dignity because we are special to God.

But if you ask what a man is, and what he can become, you need only look at Peter's namesake, Peter the disciple of Jesus.

He was a man entirely human, full of faults and failings. Talkative, thrusting, impulsive, boastful, jealous and often plain stupid.

Yet Jesus chose him, and he became the first Church member – why?

First, because of his big heart. How he loved Jesus! What enthusiasm he had, and what courage! It was Peter who tried to walk on the water. Who, another time, jumped in when John pointed to Jesus standing on the shore.

Second, Peter had such clear insight. It was he who said, 'To whom else can we go? You have the words of eternal life.'

Third, he knew his own failure and his need.

He let Jesus down, and couldn't forgive himself: but he repented and was forgiven. One day Jesus said, 'Peter, do you love me?... Peter, feed my sheep.' And from that day he became Christ's faithful soldier and servant to his life's end.

May the baptism of your Peter today help him to become, like Peter the fisherman, a true man, Christ's soldier and servant to his life's end.

The Chief End of Man

What is life all about? What is its main purpose? If you had asked our forefathers they might have quoted the old Scottish catechism: 'The chief end of man is to glorify God and to enjoy Him for ever.'

I believe that is so. It has never been put better. And this is why our children need to grow up to know Jesus as their Saviour and Lord.

Because it is through Jesus that God becomes most real to us.

This sacrament is the linking of your children to Jesus. We ask Him to bless them and He does. He took them up in His arms, we read, and blessed them; and He does it still.

And they are sprinkled with water because water is the symbol of cleansing – which we all need. We are human, and human nature has to be cleansed and transformed. None of us is fit for the Kingdom of God without this.

It is a joyful sacrament, for it contains the promise of God that we can be transformed and live as His sons and daughters. It means that a Christian life is possible for us.

May your children, then, enter their Christian inheritance. May they go on, in the old phrase, 'to improve their baptism'. May the name of Jesus be loved, and spoken only in reverence in your home, and may you know that as He welcomes your children today, so the Church welcomes them, and welcomes you, always.

Lent to God

Hannah, the mother of Samuel, so longed for a child that she made a vow. 'If the Lord grants me a child I will give him to the Lord for his whole life.'

The child came and they called him Samuel, which means 'asked of the Lord'.

Shortly afterwards they took him, with a sacrifice, into the local Temple at Shiloh.

The priest was Eli and, after slaughtering a young bull, they came to him, and Hannah said, 'What I asked I have received; and now I lend him to the Lord; for his whole life he is lent to the Lord.'

So Samuel was left behind in the Temple. Eli brought him up and he became a great servant of God.

Today we don't lend our children to the Lord in that way. But I am sure you have come here not only to have Tom baptized, but because you are grateful to God for so great a gift. Like Hannah, you may want to make some kind of sacrifice. But what?

We know now that what pleases God is not bulls and rams, and material gifts, but rather the giving of ourselves. 'What does the Lord require of you, but to do justly, and to love mercy, and to walk humbly with your God?'

Finally, there is still a sense in which we can lend our children to the Lord. This is symbolized when you put Tom in my arms and I baptize him. I don't keep him, as Eli did. I hand him back to you, for you have a part, the chief part, to play in his upbringing.

From today he is not just your child, but one whose life has been given to Jesus Christ. May the Christ who comes to him now in Baptism continue with him always.

May you want this, and bring him continually, as he grows, to Shiloh – that is, the Church of God.

'And as Samuel grew up', we are told, 'the Lord was with him.' May He be with Tom, and with you, and in your home, always.

Hannah, Samuel, and the Coat

Hannah, in the Old Testament, brought her baby Samuel to the Temple and, we are told, 'lent him to the Lord'. She handed him over to Eli, the priest, and he stayed there, to spend his boyhood in the service of the Temple, and God.

We have just sung:

> 'We bring them, Lord, and with the sign
> Of sprinkled water name them Thine.'

That, too, is a way of lending them to the Lord. Acknowledging that they are not just ours, to bring up as we like, but His, to be brought up in His ways. For Hannah that meant handing her baby over, but hers was a special case. She would not expect all mothers in Israel to do that.

And notice that Hannah, even though she had lent Samuel to the Lord, continued to serve him. Every year she made him a coat, and took it to the Temple. Every year a new coat, because last year's wouldn't do, it would be outgrown.

Every year a child's needs change. You have begun a long journey with your children, and if you are to serve them through every stage of that journey, you must meet those changing needs. I dare say you have read many an article in magazines about bringing up children – you may even have a whole shelf of books on it. But what of their spiritual upbringing, their developing religious needs? The Church is here to help you with this, both through Cradle Roll and Sunday School, and through ministering in many ways to you, the parents. Keep in touch, and let the name of Jesus, the family of Jesus, the love of Jesus be the background and the inspiration of all you do with your children and for them at home.

And may this sacrament, at the beginning of the long journey, bring you and your children the blessing and the presence of Him who gives it – our Saviour Jesus Christ.

Planting Well

Here is a verse from Psalm 92. 'Those that be planted in the house of the Lord shall flourish in the courts of our God.'

There's a polyanthus in my garden which doesn't do too well. I've discovered why. It should be in a shadier spot and in a leafy soil. You don't take a seed or a root and just plant it anywhere. You think of its needs. It may need a lot of sun, or not too much; a particular kind of soil; or space to breathe, and to spread itself in.

So with a human life. It needs the best possible conditions. The first is a good home, and you will see to that, I know. The second is the House of the Lord, that is, the wider Christian family. The family into which your Janet is welcomed today.

How true, then, are the psalmist's words, 'Those that be planted in the House of the Lord shall flourish in the courts of the Lord.' Here, in this family of Christ, may she learn to do what by her Baptism she is engaged to do today: 'to confess the faith of Christ crucified, and to be his faithful soldier and servant to her life's end.'

A New Heart

In one of the shortest of His parables Jesus likened the human heart to a house. He spoke of a householder who swept and garnished his house, and cleaned out all the evil spirits who lived there.

But, He said, if the house is left empty the evil spirits will return and bring others with them. So two things are needed. First, to clean out the house; and, second, to refurnish and re-inhabit it.

Today the water of Baptism signifies that not only our bodies but our hearts need cleansing. We ask for these little ones that God will make them pure and clean.

Should we not also ask that what is cleansed be furnished? That their lives may be filled not with the spirit of the world, not with all kinds of human aggression and pride and greed, but with the Spirit of Jesus.

One of the great promises in the Old Testament is this: 'I will give you a new heart, and put a new spirit in you.' Jeremiah called that the New Covenant. A covenant is a promise. The Old Covenant was the promise to the people of Israel, 'You will be my people and I will be your God.' But now God makes a covenant with the individual, 'I will give you a new heart.'

In Jesus the promise came true, the covenant was fulfilled. That's why the books that tell about Him are called 'The New Testament'. A testament just means a promise. When I die I shall leave a will, the Last Will and Testament it will be called – the promise of this individual to dispose thus of his worldly goods.

Well, the sacrament of Baptism declares that God's

promise is true, 'I will give you a new heart, and put a new spirit in you.'

You have brought your children because you believe there is something God can do for them that you cannot do. We want the best for our children, but by ourselves we can't give them the best. We can't give them splendid characters or fill them with the grace of God. He alone can do that. So you bring them to Christ today, and the promise is to you and to them, 'I will give you a new heart, and put a new spirit in you.'

May the promise come true, not only today but in the future. Christ does not give us a new heart and spirit, then leave us. He has given us another sacrament – the sacrament of the New Covenant, of this same promise, that our hearts may be constantly renewed.

So you have to bring your children up from one sacrament to the other. To keep them so in touch with the gospel of God's grace and love set before us today, that they will come quite naturally to turn to Him and to receive new life from Him always.

The Best Gifts

Jesus said this: 'If you know how to give good gifts to your children, how much more will your Heavenly Father.' All parents want to give gifts to their children. Some pinch and scrape for themselves to give them the best that money can buy.

But actually what *are* the best gifts you can give your children? Four of them are in the second of the vows you are going to take.

It begins, 'Do you promise to provide a Christian home for this child?' The best gift you can give is a happy Christian home. What he becomes will, in large measure, depend on his home. A newspaper commented on a television interview with Tommy Steele. He came through, it said, as a young man of honour and decency, quite unspoiled by show-biz and determined not to crowd out his private life. 'Behind all this', it went on, 'is what sounds like – though he did not so describe it – a happy childhood and a sanely balanced home life which inculcated the standards of common sense and honesty which stay with him.'

A Christian home is one with Christ's standards of love, honesty, forgiveness and service, and it is the best gift you can give.

Also you will be asked 'to bring him up in the ways of the Church of God.' I know a father who wouldn't let his children come to Sunday School, because he was afraid they would be brainwashed. What he was, in fact, doing was depriving them of one of God's best gifts, His Church. 'Christ loved the Church', we are told, 'and died for it.' Get hold of that and how can you ever withhold it from your children?

The third gift is your own example. You will promise 'so to order your own lives that you do not cause this little one to stumble.' All the Church teaches will be wasted if the child sees it contradicted at home. And you can't really give the first gift, a Christian home, without this third one, parents who themselves live in Christ's ways.

The fourth gift you can give is encouragement. You are to promise 'to encourage him later to be received into the full fellowship of the Church.' Your children, as they grow, will soon know if you don't care less how they live, or whether they ever think about God, or of Jesus Christ. The way to encourage them is simply to show them that you do care.

These are the good gifts you can give: a Christian home, the Church, your own example, and encouragement.

And now, in this sacrament, God will give you and your child His good gifts: His welcome, His blessing, His promise of salvation, and His own presence in Jesus Christ to whom we come.

The Value Given by Love

An advertisement appeared in a newspaper asking for the return of a lost teddy bear. The reward offered was £20. Now clearly the teddy bear in itself was not worth all that. Maybe I'm wrong, with prices going up, but even today I think you could buy a new one, of a fair size, for less than that.

Why was this teddy valued so highly? I expect that the longer the little girl, or boy, had possessed it, and the more worn and bedraggled it had become, the less its value would be in the market, but the greater its value to its young mistress or master.

Clearly the value was the value conferred on it by love. We talk of the infinite worth of a human being. And we sometimes assume that God loves all men because there is so much good in all. But that is to put things upside down. It is not that God loves people because they have some worth in themselves: but, they have worth entirely because God loves them. This is what gives them their value – love.

You love your baby and that makes him infinitely precious to you. God loves him and that makes him infinitely precious to us all.

As he is baptized, know that God is saying, This child is precious to Me. I sent My Son to live and die for him that he might know he is a son of Mine, and take his place in My Kingdom.

The Way the Twig is Bent

A sacrament is one of the special ways in which God comes to us, and does something for us. But you also are doing something today: what are you doing?

Well, God has given a child into your keeping, and you have come here to say that, out of all the possibilities that life offers your child, what you choose for her is that she may belong to Jesus Christ, and live for Him and be loyal to Him.

That's what you propose. May you stand by it always. There's a saying 'The way the twig is bent the branch will grow.' You are bending the twig; setting her life in the direction of God and of Jesus Christ.

'Most of us are Christians', said a great preacher, 'simply because our father and mother, one or both, were in Christ before us, and, when we were small turned our faces in His direction, and made Him a great fact to us.' We can forget that, and wander away, but there is a homesickness that eventually brings us back to Him.

Jesus once said to the friends of a sick man, when they brought him to Him, 'Your faith has saved him.' Your faith, too, can save your child. The great saint Augustine said that he owed everything to his mother's faith. 'I would not be Your child, O God, if You had not given me such a mother.'

So what you do is important: but most important is what God does.

Jesus gave us this sacrament that we might see in it the love of God. We know He loves the whole world. Today we see that He loves each one of us, as if there were only one to love. The Father of all men is also a Father to your child.

Before baby came you made preparations. You didn't want her to come into a cold, unwelcoming world. You saw there was a pram and baby clothes and everything else you needed.

Far more wonderful preparations have been made by God. His love is here to welcome Susan, His grace and help to go before her, His presence to support her all through her life.

All this God promises in the sacrament of Baptism. May she, now and always, receive all He is waiting to give.

A Precious Memory

Many years ago a memorial to Sir Walter Scott was unveiled in London. The ceremony was performed by the then Duke of Buccleuch, whose family had been neighbours of the Scotts – fellow Borderers.

'My most precious memory', said the Duke, 'is of being held as a baby by Sir Walter Scott.' Then he added, 'I don't actually remember it, but I was told it had happened.'

Something is to happen to these babies now that they won't remember. Yet, in a sense, it can be their greatest memory.

Perhaps they will ask you about it. They may say, 'Did I cry, Mummy?', and you will be able to tell them.

I hope you will tell them more than that. Tell them why they came and were baptized. Because God loves them, and wants them, and welcomes them. Because Jesus took the little children in His arms and blessed them. And because He is here, and does it still.

Not Just a Baby

It isn't only a baby that is to be baptized. It's a person, an individual. It is Alan. Someone unique in his own life, in his personality and in his relationships.

And he will have his own unique relationship with Jesus. As the disciple had who wrote, 'He loved me, and gave Himself for me.' 'God so loved the world', yes, but 'He gave His only son that whosoever believes in him' – and 'whosoever' means this one, and that one, and the next one, individually – 'that whosoever believes... should have eternal life.'

May this personal relationship, begun today for Alan, be fulfilled. May he come to say 'The Lord is *my* shepherd.' May he know not only that there is a God but the Lord is his God, and he is His child.

We must not forget, though, that he is not only Alan, but Alan Smith – the member of a family, in whose life he shares. A parent said this: 'From the day they are born my children wear my looks, share my name, inherit my possessions if any, are clearly differentiated from those not of my family.'

Alan shares in the family blessings and the family possessions. You will be asked to provide a Christian home for him, and this is the greatest blessing in which he can share.

What is a Christian home? What differentiates a Christian family? Not a lot of God-talk, but simply a home in which Jesus is loved and honoured; and in which His Spirit of love and joy, of generosity and trust, of unity and forgiveness and peace is known.

Today he is also welcomed into the larger family of the Church. This family too should be differentiated from the family of mankind. It is (or, we are) the family of those who hold and practise the Christian faith, and who look always to Christ crucified; the fellowship of the Cross, and of those engaged to be His faithful soldiers and servants to their lives' end.

The Son of a King

Two hundred years ago, on the west coast of Africa, slaves were being embarked to be transported to America. They were shuffling along in chains, and their heads were bowed with hopelessness and grief. But one young man walked with a kingly bearing, his head thrown back and his shouders squared. 'Who is that man?' asked one of the officials. A slave-driver replied 'He is the son of a king, and he can't forget it.'

Who are you, and who am I? The sacrament of Baptism answers that question. In it God claims us, and says to each one who is baptized, 'This is my child. I welcome him: and I have sent Jesus Christ to be his Saviour and King.'

Who are we? You might say we are sons and daughters of the King of Kings. And the Bible tells us that we have a high calling, ourselves 'to be kings and priests unto God.' Or listen to what St John says: 'How great is the love that the Father has shown to us! We were called God's children, and such we are... what we shall be is not yet disclosed but... we shall be like Him.'

'He is the son of a king, and he can't forget it.' May these babies grow up to know who they are. And when others lose heart, or shuffle through life spiritless, may they be seen to be different – because they know they have been made children of the King of Kings.

Into the Church Universal

When Donald is baptized I shall declare that he is 'received into the membership of the Holy Catholic Church, and is engaged to confess the faith of Christ crucified, and to be His faithful soldier and servant unto his life's end.'

What does it all mean? Well, there's the word 'membership'. He is already a member of the human family, of your family. Now he is made a member of a universal family (that is what the word 'catholic' means – 'universal'). Not just of Greenlaw Church but the world-wide family of Jesus Christ. This means that if, when he grows up, he were to go and live abroad, and there were no Church of Scotland congregation, he could identify himself with any other Christian Church without being re-baptized or re-confirmed. You might say he is grafted today into a Vine that has many branches; and that Vine is Jesus Christ.

William Temple, a great Archbishop of Canterbury, used to say, 'I believe in the Holy Catholic Church, but very much regret that it does not yet exist.' What he meant was that the Church is often anything but holy and it is far from being united. But when we call it holy we are remembering that it is Christ's Church, that He created it and is its King and Head. When He died on the Cross the disciples didn't get together and decide to start a Church. They stayed together until the risen Christ gave them His Spirit, and then the Church grew spontaneously. And, though, through our human weakness, it is still not united, the word of Christ to all the Churches is surely, Little Children, love one another, as I have loved you.

The Church, from the beginning, consisted of those who did two things. First, they 'confessed the faith of Christ crucified'. Second, they set out on a mission, as Christ's soldiers and servants to win the world.

We, as Christians, are committed to this twofold purpose. To confess our belief that Christ died for us, and for all men; and to be His servants and campaigners in our own generation.

The future generation, to which Donald belongs, will need Christ just as desperately as this one does. Today we ask that from the beginning of his life he may be strengthened by God's Spirit; that in years to come he may confess Christ crucified; and that God may accomplish in him and through him all that He wants Donald to do for Him in this present world.

As you bring him for Baptism we pray also for you, his parents. 'May God Almighty, the Father of our Lord Jesus Christ, grant you to be strengthened with might through His Spirit in the inner man; that Christ may dwell in your hearts by faith, and that you may be filled with all the fullness of God.'

The Choice is Ours

'Suffer the little children to come unto me, for of such is the kingdom of heaven.'

These were not special children whom Jesus blessed: they were just any children who wanted to come, or whose parents brought them. Not the children of devout parents, not children who had faith, not even docile or well-behaved children – just any children.

Any child is a child of God. Every child is, to begin with, open and unspoiled, just a bundle of responses. He is not yet indoctrinated or pressurized. He has not yet learned to double-think. Someone described man as 'a good thing spoiled': but that hasn't happened yet.

Now anti-religious people might well think these babies are being manipulated today. Not exactly indoctrinated, but started off in a particular direction. We should, they would say, lay off and leave them to choose their religion, if any, later on. But will they? Isn't there a fallacy there? As G.K. Chesterton said, 'If you leave a thing alone you leave it to a torrent of change. If you leave a white post alone, it will soon be a black post.'

Don't leave your children alone, then, to find their way. Give them the Christian upbringing they need. Provide a Christian home for them and set a Christian example. You don't have to force religion on them; but you have to encourage them.

And remember this. We are bringing them to Jesus and He is not going to give them one truth among many, or one way of life among other equally good ways. We believe that He *is* the way, the truth and the life. The Lord not of a party, or anything partial, but Lord of all.

He is the only one who cannot distort their living or

their thinking. He will enable them always to be as open, as natural, as unspoiled as a child: to be, in fact, their true selves.

In Baptism they are sealed with the Christian sign. Because we are made for Christ, the true and perfect man, and find our true nature in Him.

May He who blesses them today be with them always. May they be so filled with His love, and their lives be so centred on His life, that the pressures of the world – and there are many – will never move them.

So that not only now, but always, it will be said of them 'Of such is the kingdom of heaven.'

Mothers

Thomas Carlyle tells us that one of his earlier memories was of his mother praying. This is what he says:

> 'The highest I knew on earth, I saw bowed to a higher in heaven. Such things, especially in infancy, reach inward to the very core of your being.'

One is reminded of St Augustine's confession: 'I would not be Your child, O God, if You had not given me such a mother.'

Other great men and women have been able to say the same of their fathers and mothers alike.

Today these children have, in a way, two mothers. For they are received into Mother Church. The example and loving care of the Church can also, in the early years, reach to the very core of their being.

In that core God today plants His seed. Let such influences play upon that seed, in home and Church, that it will spring up into eternal life.

Our Part and God's Part

A Baptism has two parts, our part and God's. Our part is to present our children and to undertake to do all we can, under God, to provide them with a Christian home.

What is a Christian home?

1. It is a home in which Christ's name is known and honoured, and where the children know that He is their parents' Lord.

   When I say that His name is honoured I mean not in words only but by obedience. 'Why do you keep calling me "Lord, Lord"', Jesus once said – 'and never do what I tell you?' What He tells us about loving and serving one another, about forgiveness and humility and neighbourliness; above all, about faith in Himself and in God – in all this we are to honour His name.

2. Again, a Christian home is one in which the children are neither neglected nor spoiled, but given the love and security that they need. A love that is strong enough to say no as well as yes, and clear-eyed enough to see their faults. 'Love one another as I have loved you', he said. How does He love us? In spite of our faults, and to the point of sacrifice (true love always has a cross in it); and to all eternity. Our love for our children is to be like that.

3. A Christian home is one which is related to the Church. A good definition of the Church is simply 'the Christian family writ large'. Parents are not always able to come to church. Even if that were so, would your children know that you were *wanting* to come? And when they are older will you not *send* them, but *bring* them with you?

Our part in Baptism is to provide a Christian home. But Baptism is chiefly about God's part, and what He provides. He can give to your children what you cannot give: the gift of His Spirit, the promise of His presence, the means to live the best life of all, and the guarantee of the life to come. All these and, at the heart of them all, the fellowship of Jesus Christ, through whom we are in living touch with God himself.

The grace of the Lord Jesus Christ be with you all, now, as we come to the sacrament.

The Moses Basket and the Courts of God

I wonder if you have a Moses basket for your baby? When my children were babies they often slept, in the daytime, in a Moses basket, a big straw basket, on the floor.

It's obvious why it is called a Moses basket. You know the story: how Moses' mother, to secure his safety, placed him in a basket among the bulrushes, to be found by the princess, Pharaoh's daughter.

But this isn't the whole story. A great moment was when the princess gave the baby back to his mother, not knowing who she was, and said to her 'Take this child and nurse him for me.'

Today you give your little boy to God. I will take him in my arms, to signify that you are giving him, and I am receiving him as a servant of God, on His behalf. But God gives him back to you, as I give him back. He says what the princess said, 'Take this child and nurse him for Me.'

Moses' mother was to bring him up so that he would be fit for Pharaoh's court. Ours – and I say ours because you are not in this alone, the Church is in it with you –

ours is a greater task: to bring our children up so that they will be fit for the courts of God.

To bring up a child in the way that he should go is a huge responsibility. Even while you love doing it, and find a marvellous fulfilment in it, you can feel, 'Who is sufficient for these things?' But God's grace is sufficient for us. Here, today, at the very beginning He tells us this, by giving us the grace of Jesus Christ in this sacrament of Baptism. As little Robert is blessed by Jesus today, may the Lord bless you and keep you, too.

Family Occasions

The two Baptisms this morning are, more than usually, family occasions. For the one, friends and relatives have come from as far as London. You and they rightly believe that this is an important event in your family life. As the family gather round at a wedding and (as I would like to see more often) at a confirmation, so they are here today.

Again, what is very special for you, Mrs H., is that you were baptized here yourself. And now, in a sense, you want to share your Baptism with your daughter. May she also go on to share your grown faith and your continuing love for Christ and His Church.

With you also, Mr and Mrs L., it is very much a family occasion. Not only is your new baby to be baptized, but one of your boys as well; because, rightly, you want every member of the family to be a baptized member of the Church, and no-one to be left out. You want them all to have the same privileges, and that is what Baptism is – a privilege and a gift of God. We can't give it to ourselves, we can only receive it.

Why has God given us this gift? Isn't it His way of saying, You are Mine. I have set My love on you. I have given the good news of cleansing grace for you, as this water is for you. New life is for you. Christ is for you. And it is all free. As Isaiah said, 'Come to the waters...come, buy and eat, buy wine and milk without money and without price.'

We have just sung some lines which speak of God's care for us, and they are also our prayer for you today – the words:

> 'Henceforth thy going out and in
> God keep for ever will.'

After the baptism we will sing a hymn of praise, and thank God:

> 'For the love which from our birth
> Over and around us lies.'

– the unceasing love of God. The hymn goes on 'For the joy of human love'. The joy you parents know today. Perhaps you are a little nervous, but you are the happiest people here: nothing can give you more joy than the coming of a baby. Finally the hymn will refer to:

> 'Graces human and divine
> Flowers of earth and buds of heaven.'

These are the buds of heaven; their personalities will unfold, but only fully as they find their true life in God. So we rejoice with you today and pray that your children may grow up to be men and women in whom the light of Christ's goodness and love will shine.

Consecrating and Caring

You have all become parents for the first time. That is an exciting but also a daunting experience. How inadequate we feel when another life is put into our hands. It is often a time when we do some heartsearching and ask if we have the spiritual resources to match up to the vocation of parenthood.

In chapter 17 of St John's Gospel we find Jesus' own prayer for his disciples, whom He looked on almost as a father looks on his children. 'I have sent them into the world, and for their sake I now consecrate Myself.' You have brought children into the world, and are going to prepare them for the day when they will themselves go out into the world. You, too, may want to say, 'For their sake we consecrate ourselves.' If you do this today, as you take your vows, your own lives will be strengthened.

You can also take heart from the fact that the Church is with you. In our Scottish tradition the congregation are the godparents. What does this mean? It means that we care for the families and the children among us. When the elder comes round he is not just handing out communion cards: he is caring about you in the Church's name. When your children get birthday cards and, later, are invited to Sunday School, that is the Church caring. And whenever we pray for the children, your children are being prayed for; and when we pray for the families, you are included.

This lies in the future. At the present moment I'm sure you want other people to rejoice with you and to take an interest in your babies. Your friends have already done this. By providing this lovely sacrament the Lord Jesus and His Church are saying that they rejoice with you and welcome your Elspeth and your John, and that you are not alone in caring that they have come into the world.

And God Himself cares. He has made provision for them already. The water speaks of His grace which will always be there to cleanse their lives, as every life must be cleansed of sin. The whole sacrament speaks of His love for you and your children. They are Mine, says the Lord; in a hymn you sang in your childhood they are 'jewels, precious jewels, His loved and His own.'

If we had Baptisms every Sunday we would really get the message that the Church is the welcoming, caring society. Then we would not have to spend so much time trying to being people back to Church. We hope that your children will never need to be brought back, because they will never have gone away. And that through all the days to come you will be able to say, 'As for me and my house, we will serve the Lord.'

Taking it Seriously

I came across this sentence in a book: 'My baptism was largely a concession to the proprieties: nobody took it very seriously except God.' The man knew that his parents were not religious; and they had only had him baptized because it was, in those days, the proper thing to do.

That is less likely to happen now. People don't bother so much about being proper, or what their neighbours think, though there are still daughters who have had their baby baptized chiefly because their mother and their grannie would be distressed if they didn't. And there are always the rather superstitious people who look on it as a kind of spiritual vaccination: 'We'd better get it done in case anything happens to him.'

You, I know, do take it seriously: and you are not

superstitious. You know that God loves the unbaptized baby as much as the baptized one, and that if, for instance, an unbaptized baby dies he doesn't go into outer darkness but is 'safe in the arms of Jesus'.

Then why do we take Baptism seriously? Because God does. Think of Christ's own Baptism when the heavens were opened and the Holy Spirit descended like a dove. We don't see the heavens open – neither did the onlookers that day at Jordan. But God's Spirit still descends. It is a time of His special blessing. It is also a time of realization. We realize that Robin is not only your child but His. 'All souls are mine, says the Lord': and He says it especially to this soul today.

And it is a time of promise. 'Though little children do not understand these things', says the service, 'yet the promise is also to them.' What promise? The promise of fogiveness of sins and the new life made possible for us in Jesus Christ. And the promise of His Holy Spirit, which makes it happen.

There is nothing mechanical about it. Robin won't automatically grow up to be a Christian. He will have to 'possess his possessions'. The human response is necessary before the divine gift can become effective.

You, and we in the Church, with God's help, must see that the promise of today is fulfilled. That he enters into all the privileges that are before him, the life of the Church, the nobility of a Christian character, Christian citizenship, the companionship of Jesus Christ. May what is done today be fulfilled by Robin being 'filled with all the fullness of God'.

Loved and Valued

I read the other day of a Victorian girl, aged eighteen, who had what we would call an inferiority complex. 'After all the years of being snubbed by her father and step-mother', wrote her grand-daughter, 'and of unthanked fagging for her brothers – she found it quite impossible to believe that anyone should really want and value her.' And she herself wrote to the young man who was courting her: 'It seems so very strange to me that anyone can love me in the way you do. It is such a new sensation that I am worth caring for or fit for anything but just to be useful.'

To be loved and valued: it is what we all need. At village concerts, in my last parish, the audience always responded to the tear-jerking ballad 'I'm Nobody's Child' – the plight of someone unwanted and of no account struck a chord in their hearts.

Your Jennifer is, of course, loved and treasured. But Baptism says something more: that God Himself both loves her and values her. As Christ, in whom God's love is made known, both took the little ones in his arms and spoke of their worth – 'Of such is the kingdom of God.'

This sacrament, we are told, 'is a sign of adoption, and resurrection into everlasting life.' We are worth so much to God that He adopts us, that is, He chooses us to be His own. He invites us, as an adopted child is invited, to share in His own life, and to receive His protection, and provision, and concern.

A sign of adoption: yes, and of resurrection, of starting a new life. Jennifer has begun her life in your family; now she is to begin life in Christ. In her relationship with Him, and in the Church which has been called 'the community of the resurrection' she will live on another plane.

St Paul once said he was 'a citizen of no mean city', his native city of Tarsus. He also said, 'I am a citizen of heaven'. Jennifer, too, has her native city; and today she is also made a citizen of heaven.

God so loves us and values us, that He bestows this honour on us, making us citizens of heaven. It means that even now we are raised with Christ, to share in His risen life; and that when our brief life on earth is over we continue into the life everlasting.

May Jennifer come to know this: that she is loved and valued by you, and by us all, on earth; and that she is loved and valued both now and to all eternity by God who created her and by Jesus Christ who died for her and for us all.

How Do You Know My Name?

There are various stories about children misunderstanding the Lord's Prayer. 'Hallowed be Thy Name' is especially difficult for a small child, and one, for example, used to say 'Harold be Thy Name'. But I like best the little girl who gave up and substituted her own line, 'Our Father which art in heaven, How do You know my name?'

How, indeed, does God know each one of us as an individual? Isn't this why we say the baby's name as we baptize him? He isn't just any baby, but Alastair or Susan, Ian or Eva, known to God.

The Bible speaks of 'the Lamb's great Book of Life' in which our names are written in heaven. The Christian belief in immortality is not of a vague Nirvana, in which we are all like drops of water falling into the ocean: it is of a heaven where we shall know and become known.

Among the thousands of inscriptions on the war graves of the First World War, not a few say 'Known only to God' – perhaps 'A Scottish soldier, known only to God'. No-one can tell you his name; but God knows it. That is a great consolation.

Even in this life we need to be known and loved. It is a recognized fact that many young people who go wrong come from homes in which there has been no normal loving relationship. And there is the case of the infants in an orphanage who were brought up on a regular routine according to every rule of modern hygiene and diet, and with a minimum of human interference. Strangely, they pined and some even died. Then someone said, 'Why don't you fondle the babies? A baby must have love.' That loving contact with a nurse or a foster mother made all the difference.

We need to be known and loved, by our parents and by God. And Baptism speaks of the love of God. He is not a God who withdraws until we deserve His love. He does not say, 'Be good, or be faithful, and then I will love you.' He loves us before we are aware of it, and when we love Him it is because He first loved us.

So today God says, This is My child. If he is to grow well he needs to be cherished by you, his parents. And if he is to grow to his full Christian stature he also needs the gracious cherishing of God. Today it is mediated through Baptism. Afterwards you and I, and all Christian people, can be the mediators of God and of His Christ to this child and to all the other children in our midst.

A Magnificent Entrance to Somewhere

The Marble Arch in London has been described as 'a magnificent entrance to nowhere.' Is that what Baptism is? A child is baptized, then what? He is christened, brought to Christ, blessed by Christ, welcomed by the Church, and then what? Is there anything more, or is it all past and done? Through the gate and out on the other side?

An all too familiar story is that the child does go on to Sunday School and even right on to the Communicants' Class: only to drop out as soon as his name is on the adult roll. As a cynic once said, 'The last thing you do before you leave the Church is to join it.'

Of course, that's all wrong. And we pray it won't happen to the children baptized today, but that their Baptism will be a magnificent entrance to somewhere.

May it be a gate of entry to the Christian community. To be within the community of the Church is the best safeguard for your child's future. We sang the hymn about Zion's city ('Glorious things of thee are spoken'), and Zion's city means the Church. The hymn says:

> 'With salvation's walls surrounded,
> Thou may'st smile at all thy foes.'

May these little ones enter into the safe fold of the Church's fellowship. And may their Baptism be a gate of entry to a great treasure-house. To the spiritual riches that are in Christ Jesus. 'See the streams of living water', says the next verse. Streams of grace and goodness that flow from Jesus Himself. The water I will sprinkle stands for that living water, and for the treasure of the Holy Spirit.

An entry into the Christian community: an entry into the treasure-house of Christ. And also, an entry into a new status, a new relationship, as sons and daughters of God. That is in the hymn too – the streams 'well supply thy sons and daughters'. And not only are we made, in a new way, His children, we are also made kings and priests.

> 'Jesus whom their souls rely on,
> Makes them kings and priests to God.'

That is your children's Christian heritage, which they enter into today. No, it isn't 'a magnificent entrance to nowhere'. It is the entrance that leads right on to eternity.

The Master's Call

'The Master is here, and is calling for you.' These are the words Martha spoke to her sister Mary, when their brother Lazarus died. At that time of grief what a comfort it was to know that Jesus had come: and if He was asking to see Mary it meant He had come to help her.

Your situation today is very different. It is a time of rejoicing. But I bring you the same message, 'The Master is here and is calling for you.'

He is here because He shares our joys as well as our sorrows. He is here because He wants the little children to be brought to Him. 'Suffer them to come unto Me.' He is here because this is one of His chosen meeting-places with us. He is here because our children are not only ours, but God's: and He comes to welcome them into His Father's household and into His own family, the family of Christ.

You, the parents, have come today not just because it is a custom, or because the Church or the minister or your own parents have called you here. The Master has called you. The babies are too young to hear His calling them, but you have heard.

And He calls them, your children and has provided this sacrament for them. Why? Think again of Martha and Mary. The Master had come and had called them in order to declare, 'I am the Resurrection and the Life', and to raise Lazarus from the dead.

The daffodils in my garden have started to come to life. What a wonderful sight! After winter the coming of spring. The resurrection of the earth! But this is God's purpose for us all: that we should come alive, not just physically but spiritually.

So we bring our children, at the very start of their lives, and ask that He may give them His own life, now. It will remain hidden in them for a while, as the colour and beauty of the spring flowers is hidden. But we pray that it will grow in them, that their lives may be to the glory of God; that they may know for themselves that the Master is here, and is calling them; and that they may be His true followers to their lives' end.

'Baptizatus Sum'

Martin Luther, the great Reformer, tells us that when he was depressed (and he was subject to depression), or tempted, or afraid, he used to say out loud 'Baptizatus sum' – 'I have been baptized'. He was reminding himself of who he was, a child of God, and of what had been done for him and to him – his sins had been forgiven, and he had access to the Holy Spirit who is the living Christ.

Let us all be thankful today for our own Baptism for it means just this. That we are released from guilt and despair, as we turn to Christ. And that God has provided for our spiritual need, which is very great.

In Baptism, there is not only release from the past but promise for the future. Your child is 'engaged to be the Lord's'. That is a beautiful phrase. As the love that brings an engagement is to blossom and deepen in marriage, what is begun here today – your John's relationship with Jesus Christ – looks forward to its consummation in something greater still: the time when he will give his own heart and will to Christ, and be 'His faithful soldier and servant to his life's end.'

In many of us, alas, the promise of our Baptism is very little fulfilled. We settle down as 'good enough Christians' or 'ordinary Christians': not the Sermon on the Mount kind, who are to have something extra; not like St Paul who, all his life, 'pressed on towards the mark'.

No, we are not meant to stop halfway, or to be bound or inhibited by our sins. We are meant rather, to be like those Japanese flowers that you put in water. They are waiting for the water to release them, and they immediately open and expand in all their beauty.

That is what the gospel can do for us, and for the world. The promise is there when the water of Christ's cleansing grace is sprinkled on your child and he is engaged to be the Lord's. May he go on to know, like Luther who said 'Baptizatus sum', that the means of grace, given in his baptism, will be there for him always. May you teach him this, and may God bless and keep you all to your lives' end.

A Joke That's Just Begun

Do you know the line from Gilbert and Sullivan: 'Life is a joke that's just begun'?

It's a great philosophy, and when you see a baby's smile you can believe it. 'Out of the mouth of babes and sucklings...'.

'Life is a joke that's just begun.' Perhaps it's more accurate to say, that's what it's meant to be – but the enjoyment is spoiled by some perversity, some flaw in human nature. Paradise is soon lost, and has to be regained.

The good news is that in Jesus all God's promises come true. Life again becomes deliriously happy, and we can lift up our hearts and live.

So we bring our children to Jesus; to him who said, 'In the world you will have tribulation; but be of good cheer, I have overcome the world.' The path won't be smooth for your Rhona, any more than for anyone else. But with a Christian home, and the continuance of what is begun today – a continued life of belonging to Jesus – she will grow up to know that 'life is a joke that's just begun.' And that, like the small boy who went to bed saying 'Fun tomorrow!', there will always be an eternity of happiness in store.

From Generation to Generation

'God of our fathers! be the God
Of their succeeding race.'

These words, which we sang, suggest the handing on of faith from generation to generation. That is our prayer today, that your strong faith may also be your children's and, in turn, their children's also.

Faith is something we can't entirely hand on. It is like the oil which the five foolish bridesmaids forgot to put in their lamps, in Jesus' parable. They tried to borrow it from the other five, but they couldn't. You can't borrow other people's faith: you must have your own.

But your children's faith can be kindled by yours. In that way it is handed on. 'One loving heart', as they say, 'sets another loving heart on fire.' So it may make all the difference to your children that you are strong in the faith. That you have already said, and say again today 'But Thou shalt be our chosen God.'

Already, today, you are doing something for your child. You are bringing her, through this sacrament, into the covenant of God's mercy. If she grows up to know that His promises are to her, that His love and His guiding Hand are on her, and that she belongs with His people, that will go a long way towards kindling her own faith.

In the end, though, it is God Himself who will act upon her, as He does today. A sacrament is not something we do, but something God does. Jesus laid His hands on the little ones and blessed them, and God will do that now.

And afterwards? Well, we (that is, both you and the

Church) must keep the road open: must suffer the little ones to come to Him. We must see that the road between home and Church is kept open, as it is open today. Your home has come into the Church. And the Church, in its caring, its teaching, its friendship, and all its reminders of the unseen world must come into the home, into all our homes.

Then one day, not very far off, your child, and all the children baptized here, will grow up to say 'God of our fathers be *my* God', and of their own accord they will follow Jesus who already calls them, even before they can know it, today.

The Swallow's Nest

In the prose version of the psalm we sang (the 84th Psalm) are these words:

> 'Yea, the sparrow hath found an house, and the swallow a nest for herself, where she may lay her young, even thine altars, O Lord of hosts... Blessed are they that dwell in thine house... Blessed is the man whose strength is in Thee.'

In the Temple the psalmist had found sparrows, and a swallow in its nest: and it strikes him that this is right and proper. Is not God's house meant to be a home, a place of refuge for the weak and young: a place where they are not destroyed nor hurt, but are among God's people who accept them?

It is the Old Testament equivalent of 'Suffer the little children to come unto Me and forbid them not.'

We bring these little ones today to Christ, and into God's house. Here may they be nurtured like the young swallows. Here may they find their other home. Here, find acceptance and love and be at peace. Here may they dwell, and be made strong as they are taught the things of God; and grow to love Jesus and to find Him among His people.

> 'Blessed are they that dwell in thy house... Blessed is the man whose strength is in Thee.'

But the young swallows would not be there unless the mother swallow had built her nest there. If our children are to be brought up in God's house, and in the love of Christ, the parents must create the conditions, and lay the foundations and be there themselves.

May God bless you and your children, together, in His Church.

Whom Is Baptism For?

The sacraments are gifts of God to His Church. So they are not to be given indiscriminately to everyone. Baptism, for instance, would be devalued if it were offered along with a list of National Health benefits available to every mother at childbirth.

On the other hand, we in the Church cannot draw too rigid a line and say we will only baptize those whose parents are on the church roll. In the eyes of Christ, His Church will include people who, for one reason or another, have never formally joined it.

Who then are to be baptized? Not all children, but, as the Reformers expressed it, 'the seed of the faithful'. Then who are 'the faithful'? I like this definition: 'those who are in such an effective relationship with Christ that their home is truly part of the Church, and one in which children will be trained in Christian ways.'

Baptism, then, is for children whose parents are trying to make theirs a truly Christian home and who want to give them a Christian upbringing. Two tasks which we cannot perform in our own strength, but only with the help of God.

Baptism reminds me of this. We cannot baptize ourselves. It is something which we receive, which is done to our child who is utterly dependent, and to ourselves. It is as if Christ is saying, at the very beginning of a human life: Look, you need me; you need My grace today and you need it always.

We can't baptize ourselves, and we can't make ourselves or our children Christians. We must let the Spirit of God come into our hearts as He enters into this child today.

There is a danger, isn't there, that because God does so much for us, and because He gives Himself so freely through this sacrament to each child, that we may think, Our child is now a Christian; he doesn't need salvation for he already has it. We have to remember that what is given may later be refused; what is grafted may wither; what is created may not grow. What is begun here today has to be continued and nourished. In this both parents and congregation, and all who have the care of these children are called to be fellow-workers with God. But it is God alone Who plants and Who gives the increase, and Who through Jesus Christ gives us eternal life.

The Warrant

In a few moments I shall say, 'Hear the words of our Lord Jesus Christ...Go and make disciples of all nations, baptizing them...'. That is often called the Warrant of the sacrament of Baptism; just as other words of Jesus, 'Do this in remembrance of me', are the Warrant of the sacrament of Communion.

The warrant. What is a warrant? Well, if a police officer came along and said, 'I have a warrant for your arrest' it would mean he had the authority to arrest you. It wasn't just his own idea, or his own desire, but he had the authority from higher up. He had been given it.

I am going to baptize your baby, not because it is something ministers do, or like to do; and not even because it is something the Church does, or tells me to do. But because Jesus Christ himself says so. He has given the warrant and the Church is only His agent.

Why has He given us this to do? One answer is that He Himself received the authority. 'All power is given unto Me in heaven and in earth', He said. 'Go ye, therefore, and make disciples of all nations, baptizing them.' So it was with the authority He received from God that Christ gave this sacrament: and that is why your child is baptized not in the Name of Jesus only, but in the Name of the Father, and of the Son, and of the Holy Spirit.

Why has Christ given us this to do? The other answer is in the words 'Go and make disciples of all nations.' Baptism is part of the making of a disciple. If you are grown up and have never been baptized you may become a disciple first, and then be baptized to mark it, and to surrender to the grace of God. Even then you are only at the beginning of your discipleship. An infant is even more at the beginning. He has not yet made a conscious profession of faith; but you, his parents, will make it, and will bring him up in such a way that, please God, he will make it early for himself.

Meanwhile Jesus says, 'Let this little one come to me, for of such is the kingdom of heaven.' The warrant extends to him, and he is already engaged to be the Lord's.

And the blessing and the grace, the love and the welcome of Baptism are here for him now.

What a Baby Needs

How helpless a baby is! It doesn't really know what it wants or needs. It may be hungry, but it doesn't know that it is milk it needs.

Now, what would you say of parents who never gave their baby either milk or baby food? You would say that they were heartless and cruel. The baby wouldn't know what it needed, but it was the parents' business to interpret its needs.

You are interpreting one of your child's greatest needs today. You are saying, She needs God, she wants God, she is made for God. It would be terrible if you deprived her of that. Her life would be incomplete.

There is another thing she needs which, alas, many children don't have – a complete home. That is, a home where there are two parents, together bringing up their children.

I heard an authority on prisons prove, with statistics, how a large majority of offenders come from homes where they have not been brought up by both parents.

It is true, of course, that there are many one-parent families where a deserted or bereaved mother or, less often, a father, is coping wonderfully with young children, but it takes great resources of courage and character. And these need especial support from the Church.

The fact remains that, as it takes a man and a woman to produce a child, it takes a man and a woman together to understand and to bring up a child. Some go so far as to say that on their own neither can fully know the child; the father knows one side of him and the mother knows another side. And he needs the influence of both.

Your child is greatly blessed in having the environment of a happy and united parentage, and in the joint training you will give her. Because you stand here together today, and take the vows, and your Mary Jane is baptized, you will find a still deeper love for one another. May your home continue to be a blessing to her – not only from you but from God – through all the years when her character is being formed, that she may always be Christ's bairn.

Counting the Cost

In Nepal, away up on the borders of Tibet and China, an Indian pastor was sent to prison for baptizing people publicly in a river. In spite of this, the Church goes on baptizing there because it says it is the Lord's clear command; and that to be baptized is a sign and seal of belonging to the people of God. For them, it is a nailing of their colours to the mast.

You are not running any risk in bringing Margaret here for Baptism today: but you, too, are nailing your colours to the mast. And you are saying that you want Margaret to belong to the people of God – not only to your family, not only to this community, or to the people of Scotland or of Britain – but to the people of God.

Those Christians in Nepal knew the risk they took in

becoming Christians. They would be marked men and almost certainly persecuted. Here, in Scotland, people take vows easily, and often it doesn't mean a thing. There, they have to count the cost.

What of the vows you will take, to bring your children up in the Christian faith, and in the ways of the Church of God? Do you intend to take them seriously? Have you counted the cost? For there is a cost to yourselves, in your own life and example, and in your own churchmanship.

Let me put it plainly. The average churchmanship one sees in this village just won't do. You must aim far above the average. Because God requires our best. 'Put first the Kingdom of God', says Jesus. That is, get your priorities right. Like Joshua who said, in the presence of all his fellow-countrymen, 'As for me and my house, we will serve the Lord.'

As you make this resolve, the Lord will be with you, and will bless and keep you, and the joy of the Lord will be your strength.

The Sure Foundation

A building needs a good foundation if it is to stand the tests of time. Our lives, too, should be well founded: and I am sure this is one reason why you have brought your children for Baptism. St Paul told the Corinthians he had given their lives a good Christian foundation, and then he added that it was Christ Himself who was that foundation – not anything that a man could lay.

We sing 'Christ is made the sure foundation', referring to the Church, but His example and teaching and spirit are also the sure foundation of a Christian character. And these are best given through a Christian home.

One of the greatest Scottish churchmen of this century

was Dr John Baillie. He was an international scholar, a Moderator, and a president of the World Council of Churches. In a short book about his own faith he describes, with deep gratitude, how he was trained in Christian character. 'I cannot remember a time', he says, 'when my life seemed to me to be my own to do with as I pleased. I was under orders and it was from my father or my mother or my nurse that the orders came. Yet my earliest memories clearly contain the knowledge that these elders did but transmit and administer an authority of which they themselves were not the ultimate source...In other words I understood that my parents were under the same constraint that they were so diligent in transmitting to me.'

Jesus, as a child, would have caught the same spirit from His parents, and He would have understood more and more that God was His loving Father – from the things he saw in Joseph.

'Train up a child in the way he should go', says the Book of Proverbs, 'and he will not depart from it.' May the foundation laid here today, and built on in your home, as well as by Church and Sunday School and every other Christian influence, make them 'Christ's soldiers and servants to their lives' end.'

Earmarked

In a shop I found what I was looking for. It was on a shelf behind the counter. 'I'm sorry, sir', said the salesgirl, 'I can't give you that one; it's earmarked for a customer. We'll have some more coming in.'

It was earmarked, set apart, claimed. It had a ticket on it, saying to whom it belonged. Baptism is rather like that. P.T. Forsyth, a great theologian, says it means that 'the stamp of being God's property has been put on the child in a public way.' It is a sign of ownership, the sign that your child belongs not only to you, but to God.

The word 'earmark' comes from the old custom of marking a sheep's ear, as a sign of ownership. Just as any flock or herd of animals may be marked with a dye or branded.

In Old Testament days the Jews, being a pastoral people, looked on themselves as God's sheep. The Lord was their Shepherd and, as we often sing:

> 'We are his flock, he doth us feed,
> And for his sheep he doth us take.'

In the New Testament Jesus says, 'I am the good shepherd'. He not only claims His sheep, and sets them apart, but He knows them all by name. When I speak your baby's name today, it is because she is not only becoming one of the flock of Christ's Church; she is known personally and loved by the Shepherd.

And we pray that she will grow to love Him, so that she in turn will say 'The Lord is my shepherd'.

Meanwhile she is to be earmarked, and set apart for Him by the water of Baptism. And as, in everyday life, we also earmark something to indicate that it is not for general use, but assigned to a specific purpose: so God through this sacrament assigns her to the purpose of professing the faith of Christ crucified and serving Him faithfully to her life's end.

Make Yourself at Home

When someone comes to stay with us we say, 'Make yourself at home'. The Church is God's home on earth, and He says to us 'Make yourselves at home'. Especially does He say it at Baptism when young children are welcomed into His family. They are welcomed, and brought to Jesus, not just for their parents' sake, and not just in the hope that some day they will become members of the Church, but because the Church is their home right now.

A Church without Baptism would be a Church in which the children were looked on as not fully belonging. They would be welcomed, of course, but as onlookers; not quite outsiders, but like children at an adults' party.

Jesus, however, said, 'Of such is the kingdom of heaven'. They have their own place, a special place, in the Kingdom of God and therefore also in the Church.

What would the life of a home be like if the children of the home were excluded? A hundred years ago, in highly respectable families, it sometimes happened. Children they said, should be 'seen and not heard' and some were scarcely ever seen, but were banished to the nursery until they grew up.

Those days are gone, and young and old share in family life together. And they should share in the life of the Church together.

We are all to help them in this. Parents and elders in making strong the link between home and Church. The congregation who, in our Scottish tradition, are the godparents, by making them at home in the Church. The minister, by providing for them in the worship; and the Sunday School teachers by seeing the Sunday School as part of the Church.

All this lies in the future. Today Jesus simply says, 'Let these little ones come unto Me.' He puts His hands on them, and blesses them. And from now on they can grow in His love and grace.

May you, the parents, be yourselves so grafted into the true Vine, that they will be grafted with you and abide in Christ now and for ever.

A Christian Home

I shall be asking you soon, 'Do you promise to provide a Christian home for this child?' But what is a Christian home? That's a good question.

It is not just a churchy home, or one with an especially pious atmosphere, or one in which the children are overprotected from a supposedly corrupting world. It is something far lovelier than that. A Christian home, surely, is one which has three essential characteristics.

First, it is a home in which Christ's name is known and loved. Most of us don't wear our religion on our sleeves, and we aren't good at talking about it. But if your love for Christ is genuine, and your reverence for Him, it will come through.

Second, a home where the parents are His disciples, and do the things that will please Him. To serve Christ, of course, means more than serving Him at home; it means trying to do His will in your work and in the community, and towards your neighbours, both near and far.

Third, a home whose standards are His. Not the standards of the jungle, where might is right, where there is aggression and greed, selfishness and dispeace. But the standards of gentleness and courtesy, of honour and faithfulness, of sacrifice and service. A Christian home is where these prevail.

A Christian home, in these terms, is the greatest blessing a child can have. In Baptism he is also brought into the larger Christian family, the Church of God. As the Church of Scotland has said, in a statement of its belief, 'It is to be administered only when there is provision, promise and assurance that the baptized will be brought up in the family of God and instructed in the Christian faith.'

This is the beginning: and we, of the congregation, who in our Scottish tradition are the godparents, are pledged to help you in this upbringing; and the Holy Spirit, as we ask Him, will help us all.

'When Jesus Saw Their Faith'

A well-known story in the gospel is of the paralyzed man whose friends let him down through the roof; and Jesus both forgave and healed him.

That story resembles the sacrament of Baptism in two ways. Firstly, because it was in response to the faith, not of the man, but of those who brought him, that Jesus began to act. 'When Jesus saw *their* faith, He said to the paralyzed man...'.

The man was no more capable than a baby of bringing himself to Jesus; and he hadn't yet any faith of his own. But his friends believed that Jesus could do for him what he couldn't do for himself.

It is like that today. You bring your children in faith knowing that Jesus will bless them according to their need.

Secondly, when Jesus turned to the man He did not immediately give him physical healing. He said, 'My son, your sins are forgiven.' Because that was this man's, as it is every man's, basic need. This too is in the sacrament, in the symbol of water. We are offered cleansing, forgiveness and renewal in the name of Jesus, who died to redeem us from our sins; because this is our basic need.

Little ones are innocent, in that they have not yet committed any sin. Yet they inherit human nature, the natural man who, as the Bible again and again affirms, is prone to evil and knows not the things of God. We are prone to goodness, too, of course, and Christians don't have a monopoly of it. Ordinary folk, believers and unbelievers alike, are able to draw on great reserves of courage and cheerfulness, of selflessness and sacrifice when the occasion demands it.

But God's intention for us is that we should live as His sons: and that is something more than the constant struggle between the light and the dark in us, or those intermittent victories. To be worthy of Him, to be the best that we can be, to love God with heart and mind and soul and our neighbours as ourselves, we have to be dependent creatures. A baby is utterly dependent, and is the passive recipient in Baptism. As your children depend wholly on God today, and receive all that Jesus has to bestow, His blessing and His friendship, His Spirit and the promise of His help and salvation, so may you, coming like those men in Galilee with their friend, receive His healing and His peace.

Children are the Big Thing

The name Dorothy comes from the older name Theodora which means 'the gift of God'. Your Dorothy is God's gift to you. To us who are Christians all children – whether they are wanted or not, whether they have a good home or are left hungry and adrift in overpopulated areas of the earth – all children matter. Because they belong to God; they are his gift.

And when, at Christmas, God set a child in the midst, instead of coming full-grown among us, every child became more precious.

A few years ago an old lady whom they called Grandma Moses became famous in America through her paintings. In writing of her someone described her love of children. For instance, when she had a household of some pretty wild children, they turned on some taps and nearly flooded the house. 'If I were you, I wouldn't stand it', said a neighbour. To which Grandma Moses replied, 'Kids are the big thing in this house. I'd like to give them some good times to remember.'

Most of us would not go so far in indulging them, but she was essentially right. A home is not just a place where peace and quiet must reign; or tidiness; or where the parents' pleasures come first; or material possessions are the big thing. Because God has said, In My house (the house of the world) children are the big thing. Jesus also took a child and set him in the midst.

Children are the big thing, because God has said so. Also because they bring out what is best in us – love and joy, selflessness and service. And because wrapped up in them is a message of hope. We have great hopes for our children, as we look forward and wonder what they will become.

The baby Jesus looked like any other baby, but was to be the Saviour of the world.

All children, through Him, can have a great destiny. They can become His companions, His brothers and sisters, the sharers of His Spirit, and the sons of God.

Start Small – Stay Small

There's a saying, 'In order to grow you must start small.' It's not unlike Jesus' saying, 'Unless you become as a little child' or, as He put it to Nicodemus, 'Unless you go right back and are born again – you can't enter the Kingdom of God.'

All parents look forward to their children growing big. Not only in body but in wisdom, and goodness, and character. As it was said of Jesus, 'in wisdom as in stature, and in favour with God and man.'

Well, that process begins today. Today, when these little ones are open to the blessing of Jesus. (And remember, when He blessed them in Galilee it wasn't just to please their mothers: He really blessed them.)

But being blessed, will they continue to grow? And for how long?

When Jesus said 'Unless you become as a little child' – unless you start small – He was talking to the Pharisees. To people who had stopped growing spiritually, because they thought they had it made. They were know-alls, and their lives were set and hardened.

This still happens. There are high school boys and girls who are no longer open to religious teaching, who think they know it all, whose attitudes, so soon, have hardened.

How can we keep our children open and responsive, like a little child? Open to the love of God, and to the companionship and the spirit of Jesus? By showing that love ourselves. By being open and responsive ourselves.

We can go on growing, and show them that we don't know all the answers; but that we need God.

We can also bring them to Church and Sunday School where faith and worship may become real for them among worshipping people.

But the main thing is that we should sit humbly at Jesus' feet. When God wanted a mother to bring up His Son, He chose Mary. Why? Because she had that humble devotion. 'Behold the handmaid of the Lord.'

What will influence your children in days to come is not what you tell them, but what you are – as you yourselves remain small before Him who is the Father not of our children only, but of us all.

What is Man?

We have sung the 8th Psalm. The psalm that speaks of the starry heavens, and the wonder of God's vast creation. The psalm that also says:

> 'From infants' and from sucklings' mouths
> thou didest strength ordain.'

And the psalm that asks the question, What is man that Thou art mindful of him?

A great point in this psalm is that the God who made the heavens, the God, if you like, of modern science and the marvels of space, is glorified by the cry of a baby.

But why? Because the baby will become a man: because of his dormant potentiality. A seed is nothing in itself, but it holds all the beauty of a flower or the grandeur of a tree.

Perhaps you are thinking today of what James might become. Will he reach his full potential? People so often grow in body and in mind, but less fully in spirit. Because like a seed we need the right soil, and to be exposed to sun, wind and rain.

God has provided His Church that there, as well as in Christian homes, we may grow to maturity. And today James's life is planted in the Church.

And now the psalm goes further. The infant will become a man: but 'What is man that he remember'd is by thee?' Man is something special. He is 'a little lower than the angels' and 'crowned with glory and dignity.' He is chosen by God and remembered by Him.

He is not just a higher animal. You wouldn't baptize an animal, however high. You baptize a child to signify he is a child of God. The Service of Baptism goes further. It says he is 'an heir of the covenant of grace, a member of Christ, and a citizen of the Kingdom of Heaven.' And when I baptize him I will sign him with a Cross to signify that Christ died for him.

What is man? We learn what he is from Jesus Christ, and from the fact that Christ died for us. Only in relation to Him can we find our true purpose on earth, and our heavenly destiny.

That is why we bring James for Baptism now.

Procreation

Procreation! We talk of the procreation of children, don't we? It is a wonderful word, when you come to think of it.

Pro – on behalf of – the Creator. It means that when we bring children into the world we are not only propagating our own species, we are doing God's work for Him – bringing into the world a creature of His.

This is why in the Marriage Service there is a sentence which says, '[Marriage] was ordained for the continuance of the holy ordinance of family life, that children who are the heritage of the Lord, should be duly nurtured and trained up in godliness.'

'The holy ordinance of family life...children who are

the heritage of the Lord.' Yes, it is a holy thing to bring children into the world and that is why every child should be a wanted child. And they don't just belong to us: we see again today in Baptism that they are 'the heritage of the Lord'.

You have brought your child here today because you acknowledge this. You have brought him that God might claim His heritage: that He might say, This is My child. The covenant into which I have entered with his parents, through My Son who died for them, belongs to Robert too.

When Robert is baptized I will say his name. The saying of the name means that he is an individual, not just a child like any other child before God, but this particular Robert before God. I could even say that it is on behalf of God – pro the Creator – that I pronounce his name. Because this is how God looks on him today; as an individual, a special person for whom He has both a concern and a purpose.

What that purpose is you will find out, and Robert will find out, gradually over the years. But day by day you should ask that the good work begun in him here today, the coming of Christ to him and the giving of the Holy Spirit, may be continued. Baptism happens only once: but coming to Christ, receiving from Him, having faith in Him, following Him, identifying with His Church and people – these are to keep happening from now on.

Why in Church and not at Home?

I am sometimes asked, Why do you insist that Baptism takes place in Church? Why not at home? After all, if you asked the parents, and still more the grandparents, where they were baptized, a good many would say 'at home'.

It *is* a sacrament of the family, but it is also a sacrament of the Church, and this is what we are apt to lose sight of when it takes place at home. Jesus gave his Church two sacraments and I don't believe he meant one to be celebrated in the congregation (even when congregations meet in people's homes), and the other only among the family and their friends.

At the start, of course, Baptism was the admission mainly of adults to the Church. It signified the start of a new life, life in Christ, and that life was one of fellowship. If you loved Christ you loved the brethren as well. The idea that you could be a solitary Christian never occurred to them – it is a purely modern idea, a modern heresy in fact.

And so, even when, for some special reason, we have to have a Baptism on a week-night, it is not a private family affair. It is held in the Church, and one or more representatives of the congregation are present – maybe the family's elder or a Sunday School teacher known to them. These representatives of the Church welcome them in the Church's name as you, the congregation, do today.

Above all, Christ welcomes them into the fellowship of which he is King and Head. 'Jean', we shall say, after she is baptized, 'is now received into the membership of the Holy Catholic Church' – that is, into His world-wide family. 'Catholic' means world-wide, and the Church is called Holy because it is Christ's Church. He created it and loved it, and gave Himself for it. And all its failures are simply failures of our disobedience.

Jean has been born into your family. Now she is going to be received not into an institution but into this other family, of all races, and all ages, and all nations: the family of Christ the King.

Glory, Glory

When you have a baby a new love is born in your hearts, and that is very wonderful – the love of parents for their child.

You have come here because you want to thank God for that, and for something else, of which this sacrament is the expression. Not only your love, but the love of God Himself for your child. As we have just sung:

> 'Glory be to Him who loved us,
> Washed us from each spot and stain,
> Glory be to him who bought us,
> Made us kings with Him to reign.'

This is what it's all about. 'Him who loved us', who so loved the world, and who loves every living soul.

'Washed us from each spot and stain'. That, too, is what the gospel is about. We come into the world and the world stains us. There is sin, too, in our hearts. But there is the grace of God, 'grace to cover all our sin'. That is why we baptize with water. The water is the good news of the grace of God.

'Glory be to Him who bought us'. Your baby doesn't belong entirely to you. None of us belong entirely to ourselves nor to anyone else. For Christ 'bought us with

His own blood'. When the minister baptizes your baby in the name of Jesus Christ he is claiming that this is Christ's child, who belongs to Him. May your children grow up to know this: that Christ died for them, and claims them for His own.

'Made us kings with Him to reign'. These children are members of the human race, and to many who see them that is all. Today we affirm that they are something more. They have a special dignity, a kingship conferred on them by Christ. They are to be His men, His soldiers and servants, companions of the King of Kings, to their lives' end.

An amazing calling and a wonderful destiny!

No wonder we sing 'Glory, glory...'. May their glory be fulfilled, and may we all help you and them to fulfil it.

Wild Flowers

Do you see something different here today? The lady whose turn it was to give the flowers asked if she could give *wild* flowers, so she went out and collected them.

After all, wild flowers beautify God's world, so why should they not beautify His Church? They are usually only in the background of our thoughts but today they are brought into the foreground and we thank her for it.

Jesus brought the wild anemones, the 'lilies of the field' to people's attention. He pointed to their beauty and said they spoke of the glory of God.

In the ancient world little children were very much in the background. They were looked on as of little value in themselves, especially the girls: only of value for what they might grow up to be.

But Jesus brought children into the foreground. 'He took a child and set him in the midst.' They too, like the anemones, spoke of the glory of God. 'Of such', He said, 'Is the kingdom of heaven.'

We think of leading our children to God. But what Jesus was saying is that they can lead us. That prophecy in Isaiah, 'A little child shall lead them', is true not only of Jesus Himself, but of every unspoiled child. For it is natural for a child to believe in God, to trust Him and to depend on Him. It is natural for a child to pray, to talk with a Jesus who is unseen but entirely real. It is natural for a child to follow Him in its own simple way.

Even today as your child is baptized he can lead us nearer to God and to Jesus Christ. To God, simply as we focus on the miracle and the mystery of a human life newly-born. To Jesus, as we turn to Him in prayer and ask His blessing, and see Him in the sacrament He ordained. All this is done in His name, and did He not promise 'Where two or three are gathered in My name, there am I in the midst of them'?

More Than Meets the Eye

People sometimes ask for an explanation of Baptism. But a sacrament, like a great poem or a symphony, can't be explained. 'The highest cannot be spoken.' When Burns wrote 'My love is like a red, red rose', you either see what he meant, or you don't. If you try to explain it you spoil it, because you have to begin by saying that actually she doesn't look a bit like a rose.

A girl who was taking her 'A' level in music had to study one of the loveliest of Mozart's piano concertos. Before the exam she said this: 'I loved it three months ago, but now we've measured every phrase-length, analysed every harmony, and numbered every bar, I can't stand it any more.' That's the danger of explaining: you can lose the essence or explain it away.

There's a wonderful story in the Old Testament of David refusing to drink the water that his lieutenants had risked their lives to bring. He poured it out to the Lord and said, 'Shall I drink the blood of these men who have put their lives in jeopardy?' It was only water, but to David it was something more: it was sacramental.

I won't try to explain Baptism to you today. I only ask you to see this water as sacramental. There is more here than meets the eye. We receive the meaning by faith, in our hearts. Through the sprinkling of a little water we are in touch with spiritual realities, with Jesus who washes away our sins and renews our lives and provides for our deepest need, the need of His grace and forgiveness.

Many, many people have said to me what a beautiful sacrament it is. I don't think they could explain why. It is not only because of the baby. It is to do with the baby and the love of God coming together, with the tenderness of Jesus Christ and the overtones of His concern for little children and the promise of His living presence with them, and with their faithful parents, even to their lives' end.

'Me Mum Will!'

Ralph Reader is the man who, for many years, led the community singing at The British Legion's Festival of Remembrance. To Scouters like yourselves he is even better known as the creator and producer of the great Gang Shows in the Albert Hall.

A friend of Ralph's once visited his own Scout troop, a large one. At the end, when the boys went home, Ralph stood at the door and wished them all goodnight. 'Goodnight, Charlie . . . goodnight, Bill . . . goodnight, Ron . . .'. He also had a special word for many of them. Afterwards his friend said, 'How on earth do you remember all their names?' To which Ralph replied, 'But don't *you* remember the names of the people you love?'

On another occasion Ralph was in the gallery of the

Albert Hall rehearsing three thousand boys for the evening Gang Show. One small boy held his hand up. 'What's the matter?' called Ralph. 'Please, Skip, I've forgotten my garter tabs.' (It was when Scouts wore shorts and had coloured tabs in their socks.) 'Look', said Ralph, 'there are thousands of you here; who on earth is going to notice?' To which the lad replied, 'Me Mum will!'

Today, at his Baptism, Robert is not just one among a multitude of babies, baptized or unbaptized. He is Robert whom God knows by name, and loves. And as that mother would see her boy among all the Gang, so does our Heavenly Father see us. The Good Shepherd, as Jesus put it, knows his sheep by name, and if one of them is in special need, like the hundredth sheep, he will take special care of him.

All this lies behind the lovely sacrament of Baptism. And more besides. The giving of Christ's blessing, the promise of His cleansing grace, and His welcome into the world-wide fellowship of His Church.

And so we proceed to Robert's Baptism, and ask you, his parents, always to see that he knows of, and enjoys, all those benefits which begin for him here today.

Part Two

TIMES, SEASONS AND OCCASIONS

Advent

This is the season of promise, the promise of Christ's coming. John the Baptist knew that God was about to come to His people, and he prepared them for it. Baptism was part of their preparation.

You have brought Claire here today because you believe in One who comes, and who will come to her in this very service. One who, we pray, will make a highway in her heart as John made a highway for the coming of the Lord. 'The promise is to you and your children', says the Bible: the promise that He will come. 'You will know Me', He says, 'from the least of you to the greatest of you'; and this is what Baptism means, that we can meet with Christ, that even little Claire meets with Him as He comes to bless her.

The promises of God are fulfilled at Baptism, and again at Communion, and also whenever we meet in Christ's name. They are fulfilled especially through His Church.

So don't ever think of the Church as a place you should come to out of duty. Think of it as a place of blessing, where Christ comes, as we pray for His Spirit and pour the water in His name; and as I say to Claire, 'The blessing of God ... descend upon you, and dwell in your heart for ever.'

Christmas (1)

'To us a Child of Hope is born' – we say that of Jesus, and it can also be said at any birth. Every child is a child of hope. As the Indian poet, Tagore, said 'Every child comes with the message that God is not yet discouraged with man.'

And *for* every child there is waiting the Christmas message, that Jesus was born to bring hope for mankind: the hope of peace and goodwill, hope for the nations; the hope of man's salvation, that life has a purpose and is worthwhile; and eternal hope.

Suppose your children had been born into a world without Christmas – that Jesus had never been born. They would grow up without any sure and certain hope, either for the world or for themselves. And it would be a grim, bleak world.

But because Jesus was born, the world isn't like that. It has its grimness, and there is neither peace on earth nor the goodwill there should be. But Jesus came bringing a great light which will never be put out, and there is love and joy, and peace and hope, for our children.

He came as a Babe, and a baby brings not only hope but joy: the deepest joy in life to those who want him, who love him and care for him. And friends come to share that joy. As the shepherds came to rejoice with Joseph and Mary, and as we rejoice with you today.

The joy Jesus brought was not only to His parents and the shepherds. It was 'glad tidings of great joy *to all people*.' And while the papers have announced 'To Robert and Margaret McLeod, a daughter', the Bible announces, 'For unto *us* a child is born, unto us a son is given' – so that we can all love Him and rejoice.

Especially we rejoice that His name is Jesus, which means the Saviour. The very meaning of this sacrament is that He is like the water which cleanses us. He was born to save us from our sins. And so we bring your Kathleen to Him, asking that He may bless her now, and be her Saviour all through her life.

Christmas (2)

What more suitable time for a Baptism than today? Christmas is the family festival. In the Christmas story we see the companionship of Joseph and Mary in the service of their Child, as we see your companionship in the service of your child. There, at Bethlehem, as here in Edinburgh, we see the joy a child brings; we see its helplessness and dependence, and the love it needs. And we see all kinds of promise in its birth, as your children are full of promise.

Children are especially dear to us today, for Jesus' sake. Because as He was made man and glorified manhood, so also He was made an infant and glorified infancy and childhood. And when He came He was welcomed and blessed, as your child will be today; and shepherds came to share Mary's joy, as your friends and all of us share your joy now.

At Christmas there was joy both in heaven and on earth. So when a child is born of Christian parents, the Church – that is, all of us – enters into their joy and, as the poet said, 'joybells ring in heaven's street'.

With special joy, the joy of Christmas, we bring Morag and John for God's blessing. We bring them to the water of Baptism as a sign that Jesus came to be our Saviour. That is what the name 'Jesus' means: 'He shall save His people from their sins'.

And Christmas says that this is glad tidings of great joy, not the glum and over-solemn thing we sometimes make it.

May your children be blessed today, and you with them; and may they grow up to know that the greatest thing that ever happened to this world is that Jesus was born into it.

Christmas (3)

Sometimes a baby grows up and doesn't know who his parents were. Perhaps his mother had died and his father gone away. Or maybe they just didn't want him and left him somewhere where he would be found – outside a police station or a hospital, perhaps. And kind people then took him into a children's home and brought him up with other homeless children.

That happened to a little girl, and when she was three she heard about Jesus for the first time. She heard the Christmas story, and how He was born in a stable. '*He* wouldn't mind', she said, 'He had a Daddy and a Mummy.'

You want God to bless your children today. Remember that the greatest blessing He has given them is you. Every boy or girl who has good parents and a happy home is wonderfully blessed.

Today they will receive another blessing. God will light a candle of love for Christ in them, a Christmas candle in their hearts, so that when they come to hear about Jesus they will love Him.

May He also light that candle in your hearts. And may another birth take place today. As a very old rhyme says:

> 'Though Christ a thousand times in Bethlehem be born
> But not in thee, then art thou still forlorn.'

Christmas (4)

By having Norman's Baptism today, by the Christmas tree, his birth is linked to the birth of Jesus. And with a live baby here before us, and not just a make-believe baby in a crib, we are brought nearer to the heart of Christmas.

You, the parents, will also enter deeply into Christmas. You can share, for instance, the feelings of Mary and Joseph. A mother's hopes and fears; her pain and deliverance and joy. A father's concern and care; his watchfulness and pride.

There is also the delight of sharing your baby with your friends. Mary and Joseph had few, if any, friends at Bethlehem, and life was to be hard for them before they finally reached Nazareth; but God sent them the shepherds and the wise men, as if to say: 'Don't be afraid, for I know: I have made provision, and I will look after you.'

You have many friends. You also have God with you – is that not what the coming of Jesus meant, 'Immanuel, God with us?' He is with you whatever this new life of responsibility may bring.

As for Norman, he will be loved by Christian people to whom all children are dear for Jesus' sake. Not *only* by Christian people, but especially, I hope, by them.

And you will teach him, as Mary and Joseph taught Jesus, that God too is his Father. That some day, like Jesus, he may gladly say 'I must be about my Father's business.'

Christmas (5)

When Jesus was born the world was given a new chance. Men could, if they accepted Him, find a new quality of life, and think and feel and act in new ways. And there was – and still is – a chance of making a new world, a world of peace and justice and goodwill.

A child is a new beginning. In a special way the Child of Bethlehem was a new beginning, for the whole human race. And He came that we might all be new men.

Doesn't every child, when you think of it, bring an opportunity and a challenge with it? This has never been said more clearly than in Bret Hart's classic story 'The Luck of Roaring Camp'.

Into a remote mining camp in the rough old days, a hundred years ago, there came a mother and her baby. The mother died, and the tough miners were left with the baby. And they found themselves beginning to clean a room out; then to clean themselves up; then to clean the whole camp up, and to add touches of beauty where there had been no beauty before. And they began to mind their language and to change their habits, because of the baby.

A bit sentimental, perhaps. In some rough characters a baby can bring out the worst, not the best. But the challenge is there, whether taken or not. The baby is not just another mouth to be fed, but another life to respond to, and to serve. And he is a gift who brings with him boundless opportunities of new life.

God's greatest gift to us was a Child: a Child in whom a new light, a new hope and a new chance came to the world. He sent Him that we might be made, as those miners in the story were made, to think not of ourselves but of Him, that we might serve Him and love Him.

He has given you your children for this, that you might think not of yourselves but of them, to serve them and love them.

In this way parenthood brings us close to the heart of the gospel; and if we have responded to the coming of Christ then we will not be found wanting towards our own children.

Christmas (6)

What has Christmas to say to us about a Baptism? When we think of Jesus' birth we think of a fragile baby being born into an indifferent world; of one for whom 'there was no room at the inn'. The world into which your baby is born is more welcoming but it is still a tough, even hostile place for many. And all babies are fragile and need protection and care. As God provided Joseph and Mary to look after His Son, He has provided you to look after yours.

In Roman Catholic countries the figure of Mary with the infant Jesus on her lap has been an inspiration to many mothers. We Protestants pay too little attention to that figure because we are afraid of the heresy of worshipping her. But that should not prevent us from seeing in her a symbol of true motherhood, of the gentleness and loving care that should be given to every child.

But Mary soon found that caring was costly. When she became a refugee, when she suffered in hearing of the massacre at Bethlehem, and when she knew that one day a sword would pierce her own heart when Jesus took the path of the Cross.

Yes, caring is costly, and as well as rejoicing in your children you will suffer with them, and sacrifice for them.

At Christmas, though, the chief note is joy. At Christmas the angels sang, and the story is full of wonder and poetry and delight. Your heart sings too, and the coming of your baby is full of miracle and mystery and thankfulness.

At this sacrament you will also know that God rejoices with you, that His love is upon you. And the blessing of Christ is here for you, and the promise of His presence with you and your child today, henceforth and for ever.

I hope that after the Baptism you will wait till after the last verse of the hymn. For that prayer of a little child can today be the prayer of us all:

> 'Be near me, Lord Jesus; I ask you to stay
> Close by me for ever, and love me, I pray.
> Bless all the dear children in Thy tender care,
> And fit us for heaven, to live with thee there.'

After Christmas

When Joseph and Mary came to the Temple with the Baby Jesus, they gave the appointed offering of five shekels – about sixty pence. That was supposed to be the price of a slave, and they were pretending to redeem Him, to buy Him back from God. It was also a remembrance of how God had redeemed them, when He set His Jewish people free. An offering of thankfulness.

The Baby, however, when He grew up was to say 'That's not enough; you are worth far more than that; see, I give myself for you.'

Joseph and Mary also gave the priest a cage of turtle doves. That was the thank-offering for a mother's safe delivery. It was also a sin-offering, as if to say, 'We are sinners and don't deserve so lovely a gift as a baby.'

We don't give these offerings any more – the shekels and the doves. But I'm sure we should feel the same. So don't forget to say thank you to God for your child. And remember that He gives us what we don't deserve. As St

Francis of Assisi said of such simple things as bread and water, so may you say of your baby, 'Brothers, we are not worthy of so great a treasure.'

But God can make you worthy, by giving you that same Spirit that comes to your baby today. The promise is not only to your children. 'The promise', says St Peter (and these words are in the service today) 'is to you and your children', indeed to us all as we come in faith to this wonderful sacrament.

Epiphany

Today is the festival of the wise men. They brought their gifts and laid them at Jesus' cradle. You have brought your gift, more precious than gold and frankincense and myrrh. And as they worshipped Him with their gifts, so will you.

It has been said that the gifts of the wise men symbolized a man's whole life. Gold, his wealth and strength, his health and talents. Frankincense, his prayers, his loyalty and his love. Myrrh, his pain and weariness and struggle.

The two greatest offerings any of us can make are the offering of ourselves, and of our children. To give yourself isn't just an emotional thing, it is a whole thing like gold, plus frankincense, plus myrrh.

How can we give our children? By praying 'Lord, make them Yours', and by being willing to play our part in leading them to Him. What that part is is made very plain in the vows you are to take.

At Bethlehem the wise men 'rejoiced with exceeding great joy', May your joy be great today, as you offer yourselves with your children. And may you say, as Joshua said in the Old Testament, 'As for me and my house, we will serve the Lord.'

Week of Prayer for Unity

The psalm we sang (Psalm 122) is a picture of community in diversity. The diverse tribes go up to Jerusalem and are united as they worship in the House of God.

Today different branches of the Church are praying for one another, and realizing that we are all one family in Christ Jesus.

Even in this congregation we have families with Anglican and Methodist and Baptist backgrounds. But we are all one in Christ Jesus. We worship in His name and baptize in His name, and you will profess your faith in His name.

In the sacrament of Baptism we confess not the faith of the Church of Scotland but the faith of Christ crucified. I sprinkle the water in the form of the Cross to signify this. When Jesus went to the Cross it was to unite broken humanity. The unity of nations and of Churches will come as they are united to Him. There will never be a fully united world until it is united in Christ.

All this is in the sacrament of Baptism. James and Samantha are to be welcomed into the Holy Catholic Church, that is, into the whole world-wide family of which we are a branch in this place.

We have to identify with a particular Church in a particular country – indeed with a particular congregation. But these are all minor things. What really matters is that Christ died for us, and that we are all united to Him and dependent on Him through all life's journey from the cradle to beyond the grave.

We are only one branch of the Church, but Christ is

the Vine. And Baptism is an ingrafting into Him, like a gardener grafting small shoots on to a healthy stock.

May your families, and all the diverse families from every tradition, be branches of the one true Vine. Let us belong to Him and to one another not only today but always.

Palm Sunday

'Hosanna, loud hosanna, the little children sang.'

On Palm Sunday we like to think of the children welcoming Jesus to Jerusalem. He came to the city that was to reject Him, but some welcomed Him and, as you would expect, there were children. Because children are drawn to those who understand them and sheer away from those who don't. And they welcomed Jesus because He had always welcomed them.

You have brought your children for Baptism today because you know that Jesus welcomes them. It is the sacrament of His welcome.

As the years pass and they grow up, will you remember this: how He welcomes them. You are promising to bring them up in the knowledge of God. It may sound an awesome task, but it isn't. They will quite naturally be drawn to Him, if you make Him known.

Some parents think that a child needn't bother about religion until he goes to school. I wouldn't agree. As soon as your children are old enought to know about Him, Jesus can become their Friend and, like the children on Palm Sunday, they will gladly welcome Him.

Even before they are old enough to know about Jesus, we bring them into His presence now, knowing that they will be blessed and their friendship with Him will be begun.

Palm Sunday (Confirmation Sunday)

Before your children are baptized you are going to be asked to confess your faith. Actually we are thinking of three confessions of faith today.

> 'Hosanna, loud hosanna,
> The little children sang.'

On Palm Sunday children confessed their faith, when they welcomed Jesus to Jerusalem. 'The chief priests', says Matthew, 'heard the boys in the temple shouting "Hosanna to the Son of David"; and they asked him indignantly, "Do you hear what they are saying?" Jesus answered, "I do; have you never read that text, 'Thou hast made children and babes...sound aloud thy praise'?"'

Jesus accepted the faith of children; He believed in their clear unspoiled vision. It is your duty, and ours in this congregation, to keep that faith alive in our children as they grow. You bring them today because they are already His, and will quite naturally respond to Him and confess Him whenever they are old enough to hear about Him. Never undervalue the faith of a child.

Secondly, when they grow up I hope they will stand up in church as these young communicants will do today, and confess Him before men. Baptism looks forward to this. They are engaged to be the Lord's – and the promise made at an engagement has always to be publicly ratified later. Not every couple, of course, who get engaged get married. Engagements are broken, and love can grow cold: it has constantly to be renewed. Your children are today 'engaged to be the Lord's' and that committal to Jesus has constantly to be renewed.

Thirdly, what happens today looks forward not only to your children's confirmation but much further, to the time when we shall all stand before Christ in heaven and confess Him there. So also does Palm Sunday, when a small band of people welcomed Jesus as their King, look forward to a day of greater triumph, when 'every knee will bow and every tongue confess that He is Lord.' May we and our children so confess Him here on earth, that we may be among that number.

Easter

The most significant thing about this Baptism is that it is on Easter Day, the day which meant new life for the world, Christ's risen life, given to us – 'Lo, I am with you always'.

In its early Christian form Baptism was always associated with resurrection. The adult or child was submerged in a pool and raised out of the water, the symbol of rising to a new life.

Your child has his own natural life, and the seeds of his own God-given personality. Yes, but that is not enough. He can have more. He can share in this new life, this resurrection life in Jesus Christ. Which doesn't mean another life beyond death, but another life which begins here and now. Whether he were baptized or not, he might catch something of that life, of the presence of Christ, from you, or from his grandparents or from the Church. But it is too important to be left to chance.

So we bring him to Jesus today, and we hope this is the beginning; and that you will keep bringing him to Jesus until the day when you and he can worship and follow Christ together.

May you, the parents, indeed the whole family, be so alive to God yourselves that quite naturally, without any forcing, George will grow into a true soldier and servant of Jesus Christ.

Ascension Sunday (1)

It was at His Ascension that Jesus spoke these words. We look on them as the Warrant for the sacrament of Baptism:

> 'All power is given unto me in heaven and in earth. Go therefore and make disciples of all nations, baptizing them in the name of the Father, and of the Son, and of the Holy Spirit; teaching them to observe all things whatsoever I have commanded you: and, lo, I am with you alway, even unto the end of the world.'

'Make disciples of all nations.' Because all men are God's concern and His children. As well as being Ascension Sunday this is the start of Christian Aid Week, when we remember that our concern has to be God's concern, for His needy children everywhere.

To baptize all nations is another matter. This is the mission of the Church, which it hopes to achieve not by undue pressure, but by its loving witness in word and deed.

But what of those baptized (and that includes our children)? 'Teach them to observe what I have commanded you', says Jesus. To observe His way of life, the way of love and forgiveness, of unselfishness and humility, of honesty, confession and faith.

Quite a programme! But, says Jesus, 'I am with you'. Yes, and He said at the beginning 'All power is given unto me'. So we can go in His strength.

As your children grow they will meet influences that will try to wean them from Christ's way. Therefore their lives must be well-rooted. They must be strong in the Lord. How? Through the strength that comes from a Christian home; and through the Church; and through our own engagement and commitment.

He is ready to bestow that strength on us as well as on our children – He who began by saying 'All power is given unto me', and whose last word was 'I am with you always'.

Ascension Sunday (2)

When baby was born you registered him as a British subject. Today, by the sign of Baptism, we register that he is a subject of the King of Kings and a citizen of heaven.

We each have two homes: the home on earth into which we are lent for a time; and our eternal home with God.

While on earth we have many things to learn, but chiefly to look up, to see where we are going and to raise others to their destiny.

Your children, as they grow, will look up to you. Will you teach them to look up higher still, to look beyond you to Christ your King?

You will promise to bring them up 'in the nurture and admonition of the Lord and in the ways of the Church of God.' That is a tremendous task, given to parents, but the Church is there to share it with you. Use it. Use this Church, which God has given to enable us to set our affections, and our children's affections, on the things above.

This is Ascension Sunday when the special message of the Church is, Look up to Christ your King. May that be the keynote of your lives – to look up, with your children, and to worship and serve Him always.

Ascension Sunday (3)

After the Baptism we're going to sing, 'Jesus loves me'. It's not just a hymn for tiny children, but for all of us. Think what it says.

'Jesus loves me' – not just 'us' but 'me' – each one of us. Isn't this why you have come? You bring your child as the mothers in Galilee once brought their children to Jesus, because you know God loves her and Jesus will bless her. He still says 'Suffer the little children to come unto me'.

Then, 'Little ones to Him belong, They are weak but He is strong.' They belong to you, but not only to you. You hand her to me, as if to say, 'We give her to the Church, and through you to Him whose Church it is, to Jesus Christ.' And I give her back, as if to say, 'Yes, she is His, but you are the trustees, to bring her up as you feel God wants you to bring her up.'

Then in the second verse:

> 'Jesus loves me! He who died
> Heaven's gate to open wide
> He will wash away my sin
> Let His little child come in.'

He died for us and ascended into heaven, that we might follow Him there. This is Ascension Sunday when we look up to Christ in glory. Your children will look up to you. See that they look further – up beyond you to Christ the King of heaven, and to their eternal home.

'He will wash away my sin'. Isn't this why we sprinkle water? Water means cleansing. We all need the grace of Christ, all our lives, to make us clean.

And the last verse – 'Jesus loves me! He will stay close

beside me all the way.' When Jesus ascended He said, 'Lo, I am with you always'. He says it again today. You don't just have the baby 'done' and that's it. In Baptism God covenants and promises, 'I welcome you today, and I will welcome you always.' Christ meets with us today, and we can meet with Him always.

May your children come to know this. And may you know that in all the wonderful and challenging task of bringing them up Jesus loves you and 'He will stay close beside you all the way.'

Whitsunday

This is Whitsunday, the day of the Holy Spirit. It reminds us that we can't make ourselves or our children into Christians. Only God can do that.

> 'Every virtue we possess
> And every victory won
> And every thought of holiness
> Are His alone.'

You want James to grow up to be a Christian. I know you do. But what can you do about it?

You can't make him a Christian, but God can use you, and send His Spirit through you. Remember the promise 'He will give the Holy Spirit to them that ask Him.'

You can also prepare the soil. Some children are like neglected or unploughed soil. The seed can't penetrate it. So prepare your child. Make him aware of the unseen world. Let him see that your hope and help are in God.

You needn't be too solemn about it. As a wise man said, little children can play at holy things. Prayer time can be fun. Sunday can be a special day. And Jesus can be their most wonderful Friend. So prepare the soil. And keep your own lives open to God. Because the Spirit will not be given to Keith or to you automatically. The Spirit comes when we meet with Christ, both here in church and at home.

So, as St Paul says, may you 'be strengthened with might by His Spirit in the inner man; that Christ may dwell in your hearts by faith...and know the love of Christ...that you might be filled with all the fullness of God.'

Whitsunday
(Christian Aid Week)

This is both Whitsunday and Christian Aid Sunday. Is this an appropriate setting for a Baptism?

Yes. Because Christian Aid speaks of the inherent God-given dignity and value of human beings. We are to feed the hungry, heal the diseased, and raise all men into the possibility of a full life, because that is what human beings are made for.

But when the war on want is over, and everyone has a square meal and a fair chance, what then? The chance, I said, of a full life, but filled with what?

The Christian answer is that we are made for God, to live in dependence on Him, as His sons. And this is where Whitsunday comes in. We can't make ourselves truly Christian, or rise to our full stature, without the power of God.

You want the best for Keith. You hope he will grow up to be a Christian; to know and to love God. But we can't make ourselves, let alone our children, Christians. Only God can: and He can use you, the parents, to bring His Spirit to your children.

There's a passage in which St Paul says that he and another Christian, Apollos, are God's agents. 'I planted the seed, and Apollos watered it; but God made it grow.'

He can use you, the parents, in the same way. To plant the seed of faith in your children, and to nurture it.

To break up and prepare the soil, if you like. (As you, James, do with your tractor. If you didn't, the seed couldn't penetrate. It would never grow.)

This is the task not only of parents, but of us all. To open up the lives of our children to God, and to plant the seed of the Christian faith. But it is the Holy Spirit who activates that seed.

We come now to Baptism, and the seed is sown. We ask for the Holy Spirit, and for Christ to make Keith His own man, His servant and disciple to his life's end.

Christian Aid Week

Today, on Christian Aid Sunday we think of the dignity of man. Every man is a child of God, and is therefore entitled to a full life. Of which many, alas, are deprived by hunger, poverty and disease. We must help them.

Baptism, too, expresses the dignity of man. As Jesus did, when He set a child in the midst and said, 'Of such is the Kingdom of Heaven'.

Christine is your child: she is also a child of God. You are Christian parents. And she shares your name, your home, your possessions, even your character, so you want her to share your most precious possession – that is, your faith. Also the blessings which God has given you: such as the blessing of being not only a child of God but a forgiven child of God, and a member of the family of the Church. May she begin to enter her Christian inheritance today as she is baptized and blessed and her feet set on the paths of the kingdom.

Harvest Thanksgiving

One thing we see clearly at Harvest Thanksgiving is how important the beginning is. A successful harvest depends on what happens to the grown crop, yes, but also on what happened away back at the sowing. You can't have a good harvest without a good start.

In our lives, too, a good start counts for an awful lot. I can never thank God enough for the good start I had in a Christian home. We all pray today that these children may have a good start.

Well, this is a part of it: the sowing of the seed of spiritual life at Baptism; and the relationship with Jesus begun here today.

It's surely a good time for parents to ask, What kind of start am I giving my children?

The seed may be sown at Baptism, but has not the soil in which it grows to be prepared too? Many a seed sown at Baptism never gets the chance to germinate. It will only do so as the soil is prepared, as farmers prepare their fields with fertilizers.

I love the references in the Gospels to the child Jesus, and to His cousin John, growing up from their infancy. 'John grew up and became strong in spirit...Jesus grew up big and strong and full of wisdom. He advanced in wisdom and in favour with God and with man.' Surely the devout homes of John and of Jesus played a big part in this.

Stuart will become a man. 'A child is the beginning of a man.' But the purpose of God is that he should grow to be more than a man. As we often sing:

> 'Behold th' amazing gift of love
> The Father hath bestowed

On us, the sinful sons of men,
To call us sons of God.'

Through the rich soil of a Christian home, through every Christian influence, may he come to know that he is a son of God, and his life be made beautiful and fruitful. May it yield the harvest of which the Scripture speaks: 'gentleness and humility; longsuffering and kindness; patience and forgiveness; love and joy and peace.'

The grace of the Lord Jesus be with him, and with you all.

All Saints (1)

Last night was Hallowe'en. That means that today is All Hallows Day, or All Saints Day. Today many Churches remember in gratitude the Christians of past generations who have handed on the faith – 'the saints who from their labours rest'. We remember, as we have just sung, how God 'Hast all our fathers led.' It is suitable that on such a day we should bring a child to Baptism. For this is the future generation. Did we not also sing, 'God of our fathers! be the God of their succeeding race'?

In this act of Baptism God declares that He is still our God, and we are His. 'All souls are mine, saith the Lord.' He declares that as He has guided and blessed each generation, so He will guide and bless our children, and the same love is given to each one.

In Baptism the promise is renewed. And God asks for our prayers, especially the vows and prayers of the parents, that His promise may not be frustrated, but that some day this child may be numbered with His saints, and may be in very truth a child of God.

As I sprinkle the water on her brow, I shall do so in the sign of the Cross. There is no magic in that. It is an outward sign of the Church's prayer – indeed of the prayer of Christ – that the spirit of the Cross, of sacrifice and love, may be laid on her heart. That she may indeed be hallowed by Christ this All Hallows Day, and be His own for ever.

All Saints (2)

In bringing Janet here today you are saying 'She is not only our child but a child of God.' This is what Baptism is about.

The Church receives the children, and the minister takes them in his arms, to signify just this – that they belong here, in God's House. Then they are given back to you, for you are the trustees, to bring them up on God's behalf.

They not only belong to God: they are made in His image. 'Who does Janet look like?' Many of your friends will have asked that. Has she her father's mouth, or her mother's eyes? But there is this other, this inward likeness.

Jesus, we are told, was 'the image of the invisible God', 'the express image of His Father' – or, in the new translation, 'the stamp of His very being'. And we are to receive the image from Him. That's why Baptism is called a sign and seal of our adoption: we are sealed with the mark of Jesus Christ. This means that our lives are in some way to reflect God. We are called to be saints, says the New Testament, and a saint is someone whose life speaks of God. In some lives, of course, the divine image is smudged and obscured as the years go on: in others the presence of Christ becomes more and more apparent.

Our prayer for Janet on this All Saints Day is that she may go on to be what we are all called to be, a saint of God.

Immediately after the Baptism, we shall be singing a

hymn that tells of Jesus bearing 'God's image bright'. It asks that our lives should bear the same image:

> 'Let our life be new created
> Ever-living Lord in Thee,
> Till we wake with Thy pure likeness
> When Thy face in heaven we see.'

For in heaven, as John says, 'We shall be like him, because we shall see Him as He is.'

The hymn also remembers:

> 'Where our fathers glorified
> In unending day abide.'

That, too, is a thought for All Saints Day. For, as a new generation is born, and one of them is baptized, we remember those who rejoice with us in heaven, and how the generations will meet together there.

St Andrewstide (1)

This is the Sunday nearest St Andrew's Day: does St Andrew have any message for parents at a Baptism?

Andrew became a disciple of Jesus by first entrusting his life to John the Baptist. John the Baptist was in a sense his spiritual father. (And we remember also that John as a child had had godly parents.)

The day came when John pointed to Jesus and said, 'Behold, the Lamb of God!' Then he let Andrew go. The initiative passed to Andrew, who was no longer on John's leading strings but followed Jesus for himself.

The role of a parent is like that of John the Baptist. You are not going to force your children to become Christians; but you are going to prepare them for it. It is for you to say to them, not in words only but by example, 'Behold, the Lamb of God!' And, if you have brought them up wisely they may be eager to follow Him.

Yours is a missionary task. Every parent is a missionary. The greatest missionaries have never dragged people to Jesus; they have drawn them gently by sitting down beside them, knowing them and loving them, as you will do with your children.

In this task of pointing your children to Jesus, God will not leave you on your own. This sacrament means that He is seeking your child too. Already He says, 'This is My child, whom I love, and whom I welcome into the Church of My Son.'

St Andrewstide (2)

This is St Andrew's Sunday, and I think of parents today as, in a special way, linked with St Andrew. Because Andrew was the disciple who was always introducing people to Jesus. He brought his brother, Peter; he brought the boy with the loaves and fishes; and when some Greeks said to Philip, 'Sir, we would see Jesus', it was Andrew, the introducer, whom Philip brought to them.

Perhaps you couldn't put into words why you have brought your children for Baptism. But I'm sure it's because you want to bring them to Jesus. That is what you are doing, introducing them to Jesus; and He is here, waiting for them. He will bless them and start a relationship with them which is like no other relationship. If our most precious human relationships, with husband or wife, parent or brother or friend, can affect our lives, and shape them and change them; if that happens, and it does – how much more character-shaping is our relationship with Jesus Christ!

By bringing your babies today, and by bringing them and encouraging them later on, so that the grace and goodness that flow from Jesus have a chance of reaching them – by doing this, you may be shaping their eternal destiny. And some day your children, like those of a mother in the Bible may 'rise up and call you blessed'.

So, as we sang:

> 'We bring them, Lord, and with the sign
> Of sprinkled water name them Thine.'

And as we prayed in that hymn, we pray again:

> 'Their souls with saving grace endow,
> Baptize them with Thy Spirit now.'

At a Children's Service

Boys and girls always love a Baptism. But suppose I asked you, 'What is happening?' – what would you say? Someone might say, 'The baby is being named.' No, that's not it, because he has a name already.

Or someone might say, 'Water is sprinkled on him.' Yes, but why? Have you ever wondered why? Well, what does water do, or what do we do with water? We drink it; yes, but what else? Wash with it – yes, that's it. The few drops I'll put on baby's head won't wash him very much, but that is what it means. It means that we all need to be washed, not just outwardly on our bodies, but inwardly in our hearts by Jesus. You all know the hymn that says, 'He will wash away my sin, Let His little child come in.'

But, good gracious, little Robbie hasn't sinned; how can his sins be washed away? The answer is that Jesus has washed away our sins by dying for us, and He died for Robbie too. So that one day Robbie can grow up and learn that all his sins (and he'll have them later on, as we all do), that all his sins are already washed away. I sprinkle the water today as a sign that Jesus already loves him so much that He died for him, to forgive his sins.

What else is happening? Well he is being made a member of the Church. Does that sound strange? Won't he have to grow up and choose to be a member, if he wants to be? But, you know, Jesus once said, 'You have not chosen me, but I have chosen you.' We can't really make ourselves members of the Church; our parents can't do it for us, and I can't do it for anyone. It is Jesus who does it. Some day if Robbie says, 'I want to join the Church', what he really means is, 'Jesus has already brought me into His church when I was a baby and now I want to say "Yes" again. My parents said it for me, and I want to say it for myself.'

Today Robbie's parents have brought him here. But it was Jesus who told us to provide this ceremony, this sacrament of Baptism, we call it, for His children. It is Jesus who tells the ministers to tell the people to have their children baptized. It is Jesus who puts it into the hearts of the parents to bring their baby.

So, you see, what is happening to Robbie is a great honour. Jesus has chosen him and is bringing him into His Church. Someone said, 'We must be planted if we are to grow.' Jesus wants all His children to be planted here in His Church, that we may grow to love and serve Him. May Robbie and may we all, as we grow up, look back to the day we were baptized and say, 'Jesus blessed me and honoured me so much then – so what can I do for Him now?'

At a Sunday School Service

What was one of the first prayers you ever said? Wasn't it this: 'God bless Mummy and Daddy and make me a good boy (or a good girl), Amen'?

It's an excellent prayer. It says '*Make* me a good boy', because that's something I can't do by myself. I want to be good, and I also want to be bad. There's a battle going on inside us all the time. Who will win? Well, if I ask God to make me good, He can send His own Spirit into my heart, and goodness will win.

When these babies are baptized we are going to ask that God's Spirit may come to them, and be in them. So that they can grow up and be good people. We want them to be healthy and strong, of course, and as wise and happy, and even good-looking as possible. We want them to have gifts of music and friendship. We want them to be good at sports and clever with their hands as well as their brains. Oh, there's so much we want for them.

But what's the best thing of all? I'll tell you what Sir Walter Scott, the great writer, thought it was. When he lay dying, his son-in-law, whose name was Lockhart, came into the room, and Scott said, 'Be a good man, Lockhart. Be religious, be a good man. Nothing else will give you any comfort when you come to lie here.'

So that's why we baptize the babies. Because we can't make them good: only God can, and we want them to be His children and the friends of Jesus from this day on. And may Jesus be with them always.

A Family about to Emigrate

You are soon to go overseas. It is fitting that you should come back here, to your own Church, before you go and, should bring your baby for Baptism. You are storing up precious memories to take with you to a strange land. You are doing more than that; you are committing yourselves and your little girl to the Lord Jesus who will never leave you nor forsake you, wherever you are.

When Fiona grows up she will learn that she belongs to His Church. It will be a different denomination in Norway, and in a different language. That will be harder for you than for Fiona, for she will be bilingual and will adapt easily. But remember that today she is not just being baptized into this congregation, or into the Church of Scotland, but into the Holy Catholic Church. That means the world-wide Church, the whole family of Christ on earth. And that is where we all belong. With all who love the Lord Jesus, in whatever ways they worship Him and wherever they may be.

We sang Psalm 8 just now: the psalm that asks:

> 'What is man that he
> remembered is by Thee?'

The most wonderful thing about man is that God remembers him, and knows him, and loves him. And God is everywhere.

The sacrament of Baptism says this too. We bring Fiona to Someone who knows her already and loves her, and has provided, in Jesus Christ, for her salvation. We all need forgiveness and new life, and by the symbol of water and the gift of the Holy Spirit God tells us that He provides them.

May God go with you, and dwell with you. And as you all become more and more proficient in a new language may you also continue to know yet another language – the language of heaven, the understanding of spiritual things. It is a closed book to many, but here, in this sacrament, it speaks to our hearts and through simple actions and the words of Jesus we see the love of God.

May Fiona always belong to the family she enters today, Christ's universal family, and come to know that wherever she is, and wherever you are, she and you are safe in the arms of Jesus, who takes her in His arms to bless her now.

A One-Parent Family

One of the loveliest moments in Handel's *Messiah* is when the alto sings, 'He shall feed His flock'. The words are from Isaiah: 'He shall feed His flock like a shepherd: He shall gather the lambs with His arms, and carry them in His bosom, and shall gently lead those that are with young.'

These words tell us three things about God, three thoughts to be treasured at this Baptism.

First, they speak of His provision for us. 'He shall feed His flock.' On the well-pastured Scottish hills you can leave the flock to feed themselves; but on the more barren hills of Israel they had to be led to the good pasture. Without the shepherd to take them there they would go hungry. And so it is with us. God knows our need and has provided for us. That is why we have the sacraments. Here at the font is the beginning of His spiritual provision for your child. And here is the promise of blessings to come; of the forgiveness and grace, and of the water of new life which are there for us at every step of the way.

Second, the verse speaks of God's special love for the little ones. 'He shall gather the lambs with His arms, and carry them in His bosom' – as Jesus did when He blessed the children in Galilee, and as He will do today.

And, third, there is God's care for the mothers. 'He shall gently lead those that are with young.' Which is also translated, 'He shall lead the ewes to the water.' It may mean the ewes that are carrying lambs; it could also mean, the ewes along with their new-born lambs. The picture, in either case, is of the gentleness of God and how He looks after those who most need His care; and that includes the mothers as well as their offspring; and surely, most of all, the mothers, like yourself, of a single-parent family.

You have come here to have your baby baptized and blessed. But, remember, there is also a special blessing here for yourself. God knows that, as a mother, you will need more courage, wisdom and understanding, more Christian grace, more resources of love and prayer and more of the water of life than you have ever had before. He knows it, and He will care for you, and gently lead you, along with your treasured Jennifer.

We, too, as Christ's people, will care for you in His name. May our prayers and our fellowship, and above all, the presence of Christ our Saviour, go with you always.

A Parent and Child Together

We are about to baptize not only a baby, but the mother as well. In our Church, infant Baptism is the norm and adult, or believers', Baptism the exception; but, of course, it was not always so. Right at the beginning whole families were baptized together, and that must have been a happy sight. As this is a happy sight today.

We do have adult Baptisms from time to time, but most people are shy about it. They need not be. Because many folk, for a variety of reasons, have missed out on infant Baptism. Maybe the mother or the baby was ill, or the father away at sea, or in the army, and by the time they got round to it the baby seemed too big. Or maybe the parents didn't believe in it, or one was a Baptist, or a Catholic, or a Jew and didn't want a Presbyterian Baptism, so they compromised by having none at all!

Anyhow, if anyone here is unbaptized there is no stigma attached. We welcome you all the more, Mrs Anderson, because you have been willing to nail your colours to the mast, as it were, before us all. You are indeed 'confessing Christ before men'. And before you and Mr Anderson promise to bring Christine up in the Christian faith and the Christian way, you will take your own vow, and declare that you repent of your sins and with God's help will serve Christ in the fellowship of His Church.

'Repent and be baptized' – that was the call of the apostles when the Church first went out to win the world. And none of us can say, 'I belong to Christ' without also saying, 'I am not worthy to belong to Him'; so we repent of our unworthiness and turn to Him for help.

Repentance means not only ‘turning from’ but ‘turning to’. Not only renouncing our sins but, like St Paul, ‘forgetting the things that are behind and pressing on’, turning our faces and our lives towards Christ our Saviour.

As you repent, you will be baptized – you and Christine; and it will be exactly the same for you as for her. Because Baptism is not what we do, but what is done to us by Jesus Christ. May His Spirit descend upon you both, together, and dwell in your hearts for ever.

A Handicapped Child

Those who are well, said Jesus, have no need of a doctor; only those who are sick. For us, this means that if our souls were in sound health we would have no need of the Good Physician. But we do need Him, from the beginning of our earthly life, and the healing grace of Christ is here for us – hence the sacrament of Baptism.

Jesus also said those words to explain why He ministered to the disadvantaged, the poor, the sick, the lame and the outcasts; and why they turned to Him more eagerly than the privileged who thought they had no need of Him.

Your little John, being handicapped, is among the disadvantaged; though, thank God, he has what many children are without, the advantage of a Christian home, and the family of this congregation which will cherish him greatly. By his very disability he is in a special way one of Christ’s bairns, and as he grows he may respond all the more eagerly to Him.

As he grows up he may have personality problems and work problems, but he will find much help. How heartening it is to see all the understanding care for the disabled that there is today.

We live in a world in which things go wrong. If they did not, if God were to prevent these accidents of birth that happen to so many, it would be a different world; an earthly paradise. But we would become callous and uncaring, for we are not ready for that yet.

A part of John's purpose in life is to help us all to care. 'Caring is the thing', said a Christian teacher, 'and Jesus taught us to care.' Only in this way will we be made ready for the world to come, in which all that is wrong will be done away; and for that day when John's spirit will inhabit a new body, the resurrection body which is without weakness or blemish.

We commend you to Christ's love, and to that promise by which St Paul came to terms with his own irremovable disability: 'My grace is sufficient for you'.

So we bring John to the water of Baptism, and to Christ's keeping.

At the End of a Ministry

I find that in the last twenty years I have baptized more than seven hundred babies. Seven hundred children were brought to Jesus Christ in this Church. They were claimed by God and engaged to be Christ's faithful servants. How has this been fulfilled, I wonder? In most cases we shall never know.

Or think of the parents. Well over a thousand parents have professed their faith, and their intention to bring their children up in Christian ways. How many parents have fulfilled these vows? In most cases we shall never know.

But God knows. And the Church goes on baptizing in faith, trusting people as Christ trusted his disciples.

There's an old legend about the Devil coming to Jesus

after His ascension and asking Him, 'What provision have you made for the future of your kingdom on earth? Have you left behind a great organization, or drawn up a constitution for your Church, or established a world movement?' 'None of these things', said Jesus. 'I have only chosen a few men, and I am trusting them.'

We, too, can only trust. We are trusting you, the parents, today, to see that what is done and said in this sacrament is not forgotten, but fulfilled.

As well as trusting His disciples Jesus continued to support them. At every step of the way they were sure of His presence, and were inspired and led by His Spirit. In the exacting and often exhausting task of bringing up children you can be sure you are not alone. Parenthood requires unselfishness and involves sacrifice. Some parents begrudge these demands. But if you joyfully accept them you will enter into fellowship with Him who pleased not Himself but lived for others. And as He had a joy which no man could take away from Him, you too will know some of life's deepest joys.

As for your children, who can say whether they will remain followers of Christ? Their future isn't written yet. But you, and we in the Church, can help them to write it. We can help them as Christ helped His disciples, by trusting them, and providing for them, and by making them aware of His never-failing love and His joy.

There is a simple prayer which asks for just this. It says, 'Bless all children in their homes, that they may have the trust, affection and untroubled joy which is their rightful heritage.'

A Prayer at the Font

Send Your Holy Spirit upon us, O God, and bless this water that it may signify the washing away of sin, and that those baptized therein may be born again to eternal life and receive the fullness of Your grace.

Lord Jesus, the Good Shepherd, take them into Your flock, and tend them always.

Amen.